PETRA

IN HISTORY AND PROPHECY

All Scripture references are from the King James Version of the Bible unless otherwise stated.

PETRA IN HISTORY AND PROPHECY
© 1991, 2003, 2009 by Noah W. Hutchings

All rights reserved. We encourage the use of this material; however, in order to protect the contents from change, neither this book, nor any part thereof, may be reprinted in any form without written permission from the publisher, except for brief excerpts used in magazine reviews, etc.

Printed in the United States of America

Published by:
BIBLE BELT PUBLISHING
P.O. Box 100 ✦ Bethany, OK 73008
405/789-1222 ✦ 800/652-1144 ✦ FAX 405/787-2589
www.swrc.com

ISBN 0-9744764-0-4

PETRA
IN HISTORY AND PROPHECY

Dr. N. W. Hutchings

TABLE OF CONTENTS

FOREWORD

In the pages of this book we are about to discover the third most famous city of the Bible. I promise you it will be more than interesting; it will be an exciting experience. The city of most frequent biblical mention is, of course, Jerusalem. From that well-known but soon to be utterly famous metropolis, Christ will one day rule the world. To the city of David will come ambassadors from every nation on earth. There they will seek favor from the Great King, our Lord Jesus Christ.

The second most well-known biblical city is Babylon. This doomed metropolis was built on the twin ideologies of culture without God—"Let us make us a name"—and religion without the Lord—"Let us build a tower that will reach to heaven." Babylon and its ideology progressively subverts the world and has arrived at near totality in our time. There is coming one single day, perhaps soon, in which the cry will go out, "Babylon the great is fallen, is fallen."

But there is another city that is most provocative as well. Remember the name "Petra"—we will be hearing much more of this most provocative metropolis in the days to come. Through the centuries it has been the crossroads of much activity in the Middle East by armies, trading caravans, religious organizers, and fleeing fugitives aplenty. It became important in the lives of the

Hittites, of Jacob and Esau, of Israel, of the Arabians, of the Persians, as well as the Greeks and the Romans. The Edomites made it their capital, and fleeing warriors from many nations their hiding place. Petra, also identified with nearby Bozrah, has been visited by thousands of religious pilgrims who have been astonished at the "rose-red" city sequestered in that improbable place.

But the past of Petra is only a prelude to its coming significance as the last days come upon us. Conservative Bible scholars hold that Petra will yet be the city of deliverance, the defensible hiding place for the deliverance of His people Israel. Betrayed and then persecuted by the Antichrist, Israel will then be preserved, delivered by its newfound Lord. Indeed, the story of Petra's past and its provocative future will fascinate every thoughtful Christian.

Noah Hutchings presents to us the account of that past and this future in this book. It will be read with singular fascination and great profit by everyone who would know the connection between history and the Bible and who takes seriously the prophetic Word. Noah Hutchings has given us significant books in the past on Christian theology, Bible doctrine, and sacred history, and has done exceptional work in the field of biblical prophecy. From the background of broad and correct biblical understanding, he now presents to the church his latest work on the city of Petra. I am sure that no reader will be anything but profited by carefully considering this book. We do well to read it with the Bible in the other hand and a newspaper nearby. Each reader will appreciate anew the consonance between these sources of information. We are promised that the pages of the prophetic Word will be made increasingly plain as we move toward the end of the age. This book, in the providence of God, will be a part of the fulfillment of that promise.

—David Breese, President
Christian Destiny, Inc.

THE MOST FAMOUS
GHOST TOWN ON EARTH

M ost tourists who visit the ancient city of Petra will surely agree that it is the most amazing "ghost town" on earth. We have seen the pyramids of Egypt, the temples of Luxor and Karnak, the Parthenon, Delos, Ephesus, Knossos, Babylon, Nineveh, Ur, and hundreds of other sites and cities of antiquity, but nothing surpasses the beauty and splendor that must have belonged to Petra. And because many of the temples and dwellings were carved out of sandstone rock cliffs, the physical aspects of this Edomite metropolis remain for the visitor's appraisal and inspection today.

Petra is located approximately 180 miles south of Amman and 75 miles north of Aqaba in Jordan. Its biblical names are Mount Seir and Sela. Mount Hor is also associated with the general area in Scripture. Petra is also described by the prophets as the rocky nest of the eagle, the city of Esau, and the stronghold of the Edomites. Few Christians realize just how many times Petra is mentioned in the Bible, and the important role it played in biblical history. Even fewer realize that God is preparing to resurrect this historical ghost town to serve as a hiding place for Israel. In this study, we will show beyond reasonable doubt that Petra will be the place of safety that one-third of the Jews will escape to from the wrath of Antichrist. Therefore, we believe these dissertations on the place of Petra in history and prophecy are of great importance.

Most visitors and tourists to Petra today are Americans who go there because of the relation of the city to Bible history and prophecy. To get to Petra, tourists usually go as members of a group, and enter Jordan one of two ways—either by airplane to the airport at Amman, or through Israel by way of the Allenby Bridge checkpoint. It is usually necessary to stay overnight at a hotel in Amman, and there are now several five-star hotels in the Jordanian capital, almost as good as can be found anywhere. The journey to Petra the following day can be negotiated one of two ways. The most economical way is by bus via the King's Highway, or the Desert Road. However, by motor vehicle it is a four-hour journey through a semidesert area void of any worthwhile scenery save a few wandering camels and an occasional Bedouin tent. After straining for an hour or two to locate some landmark of interest, the traveler usually has to settle for a nap or find something to read. I recommend a route that is quicker and more scenic. From Amman, take the early morning Jordanian airline flight to Aqaba. Flying time is only about thirty minutes. An air-conditioned bus will pick the Petra-bound tourists up at the airport, and instead of a four-hour monotonous trip, the traveler will be treated to a ninety-minute journey of mountainous fantasy. Much of the trip from Aqaba parallels a flat depression which appears to be from one to three miles wide. This plain is dotted with pyramid-shaped geological formations, and in the evening twilight, an eerie and ethereal appearance is projected. When Lawrence of Arabia passed through this area in World War I, he named it the

Valley of the Moon. It was through this unusual valley that Moses led the children of Israel up to the gates of Petra when the king of Edom refused them permission to pass through to the King's Highway that led from the mountains of Gilead that overlooked the Promised Land.

By taking the trip to Petra from Aqaba, more time is allowed for sightseeing. Aqaba itself is located on the Gulf of Aqaba, a beautiful spot for swimming and sunbathing, with a large and comfortable hotel adjacent to the beach.

The Ciq

The city of Petra is entered through one of the most fantastic rock formations on earth—El Ciq. About two miles from the entrance to the Ciq is Ain Musa (the Spring of Moses). At one time, water from Ain Musa was carried into the city by tile pipe inlaid in the rock walls of the Ciq. Some of these tiles are still embedded in rock, and the channel that was chiseled in the cliffs is still very much in evidence. We shall consider the possibility that Ain Musa is actually one of the two rocks that Moses struck to bring forth water later in this study. It is remarkable that at the peak of the Mount Seir mountain range in the desert area, springs of pure and sweet water pour from rock formations. According to *The Sarcophagus of an Ancient Civilization,* the water lines and channels that diverted water from Ain Musa and other springs in the area are of Roman construction; however, we can be sure that prior inhabitants of Petra also availed themselves of these valuable water sources.

A diversion dam at the entrance to El Ciq channels water away from the city. During the centuries of habitation by former civilizations, the dam protected travelers going to and from Petra. Although rainfall in the area is only a few inches annually, at times cloudbursts create floods that sweep through the Ciq, drowning anyone caught in its path. A traveler to Petra in 1847, Harriet Martineau, described being caught at such a time:

> Within three minutes, before I had put off my wet clothes, I heard a shout: the torrent had come down. Down it came, almost breast-high, rushing and swirling among the thickets and great stones in the watercourse, giving us a river in a moment, where we had never dreamed of hoping to see one!

The Wadi Musa acts as a funnel to send a torrent of waters, often ten feet deep, cascading down through El Ciq into the city. Anyone with the misfortune of being caught in the passageway is either drowned or pummeled to death on the sides of the rocky cliffs.

When I first went to Petra in 1978, there was one small hotel to accommodate the few tourists who came to see this ancient city of Esau. At the updating of this book in 2009, there are seventy–three hotels in Petra (some of them are five-star). These hotels alone would be sufficient to provide shelter for the sizeable population of Israel in the last half of the Tribulation. The increase in the number of hotels in the area also indicates the rising interest in Petra throughout the world.

Bedouins resided in Petra while furnishing horses to the tourists until the late 1980s. The government of Jordan built apartments for these fiercely independent people, but then the Bedouins put their livestock in the apartments and returned to their traditional tents.

At one time, the tourist had the option of either walking through the Ciq into the city or renting a horse from one of the Bedouins for a few dollars. Since the Petra area came under United Nations authority in the late 1990s, riding horses through El Ciq by individual tourists is forbidden because of environmental concerns. However, those unable to walk in and then walk out may rent a horse carriage. It is highly recommended that the visitor pay the few extra dollars for the carriage if he or she has a health handicap.

The Ciq itself is six thousand feet long, and even though a healthy male or female may make their way to the city, coming back is uphill and the climb exceedingly tiresome, especially if the trip is made in the summer. The Ciq is from about thirty feet to twelve feet wide at its broadest and narrowest points, and the sides are made of almost perpendicular cliffs, from three hundred to five hundred feet high. Temperatures in the Ciq commonly climb to over one hundred degrees in the summer and, with no wind, the heat can be unbearable. On one occasion, we allowed several people to walk through the Ciq, but then we had to take horses in to bring them out.

Just to travel through the Ciq is an unforgettable experience in itself. It is as if some master sculptor rearranged the landscape and sculpted the cliffs so that with each turn in the narrow defile, the viewer is greeted with a scene more fantastic than the previous one. By the time the visitor passes through the narrow gap into the city itself, he has been so immersed in beauty and so inspired by one awesome scene after another, that he is totally incapable of mentally absorbing another turn in the gorge. Along the way, in the rocky ravines that split off the Ciq, and high up in the cliffs, cave dwellings that are thousands of years old can be seen. The entire Petra complex, including the Ciq, is roughly twenty squares miles in size.

The City

One of the source books we used for research on Petra

is *The Sarcophagus of an Ancient Civilization* by George Livingstone Robinson, published in 1930. He writes:

> The place is situated in Mount Seir, a little east and north of the watershed of the "Arabah." The city-site is a large trapezoidal area. . . . It is bounded on all sides by high and richly colored sandstone rocks, in which there are almost countless cavities, elaborately carved, which may in some cases have been used as dwellings, but for the most part more probably were temples, or tombs. Language falters as it attempts to describe the majestic grandeur and variegated beauty of this "Wonder of the Desert."

An artist named Roberts confesses in his journal:

> I did not expect too much surprise at Petra after seeing Thebes in Upper Egypt. But the whole is far beyond any idea which I had formed of it in both imagination and situation. The entire valley is strewed with ruins, the architecture being a combination of Egyptian, Greek, and Roman. I am more and more bewildered with the aspect of this extraordinary city. Though the ruins of Karnak are immense, they sink into insignificance when compared with these stupendous rocks. I often threw aside my pencil in despair of being able to convey any idea of the scene.

More recently, a missionary from Syria described his impressions as he approached Petra from the northeast, using language in describing the environs that savors somewhat of the grandiloquent; he said:

> Suddenly there burst into view a wonderful mass of

castellated peaks, domes, and pinnacles, and other fantastic shapes, with indescribable coloring from snow white at the base to purples, and yellows, and crimsons higher up; bathed and transformed in the brilliant sunshine till it seemed like a fairyland. We gazed enchanted; for, somewhere in the heart of this brilliant mass lay the ancient city of Petra, about which we had read and dreamed, and were now to see it with our own eyes.

When carefully explored and studied, the ruins of the city give the impression of a vast necropolis. Innumerable tombs and temples, rather than dwellings, confront the beholder as he continues to gaze in speechless amazement! Mortuary chapels and elaborate mausolea command the more conspicuous terraces. Hidden in the recesses, or so elevated as to be invisible from the level of the actual city, sanctuaries called by the ancients "High Places" dot here and there the whole. No other place in all the region of Esau's possible migration so completely satisfies what is related in history of Edom and the Edomites.

The Geography

The reasons that Petra became an important city and stronghold in the Middle East are that:

» It was a water source in the midst of an otherwise rugged and desert region.
» It was situated in a valley surrounded by almost impassable mountains and cliffs, with the only entrance a narrow gorge that could be defended against any invader with only a few hundred men.
» Its colorful sandstone cliffs were perfect for carving elaborate habitats.

» It was an ideal trade and commerce exchange post for caravans traveling between Arabia, Ethiopia, Egypt, Israel, Syria, and even China and southern Europe.

When and how the unique geography of the Petra region was shaped is uncertain. One Jordanian guide informed us that the city was built inside an extinct volcano, and the Ciq was formed when a subsequent earthquake cracked the volcano's wall. There are rock formations in the region that do appear to have been the result of volcanic activity. Also, a few miles to the east there are huge fields of small pumice stones, indicating extensive volcanic activity. It has been proposed by some that these pumice stones, also called brimstone, were the result of the Sodom and Gomorrah catastrophe.

The African-Syrian Rift runs north and south just to the west of Petra, a distance of only about ten miles. The rift extends northward, creating the Arava Valley, a flat, sandy, or sandy-salt area about one mile wide running from the Gulf of Aqaba to the Dead Sea. On either side of the rift there are a host of magnificent geological wonders, including Ramon Crater, Solomon's Pillars, and the Dead Sea. Petra is just one of the many unique places in the region created when the land mass was broken up into plates as mentioned in Genesis 10:25. Within just a few miles, the elevation drops from five thousand feet at Petra to thirteen hundred feet below sea level at the Dead Sea.

From a book published by the U.S. Printing Office titled *The Hashemite Kingdom of Jordan,* we read:

Fractures of the earth's surface are evident in the great geological rift that cuts like a trench across the whole length of the country near its western borders. This system has been the scene of repeated earthquakes whose destructive power is attested to by the ruins of temples and other buildings of antiquity to be found throughout the country.... There are extensive fields of broken lava and basaltic rock. In places, the lava is classed as fairly recent, but there has been little volcanic activity in the historical past.... [The] sill, formed from limestone under a special climatic regime of ample winter rain and severe summer drought, is low in humus content but is enriched by iron oxides and silica... which gives it a red color that becomes yellowish in areas of high rainfall.

It would appear that there is a basis for the belief by some that Petra was formed by a combination of volcanic and earthquake activities. The unusual coloring of the stone cliffs and building facades is due to iron and silica reacting to either the heavy winter rainfall, or upward water seepage from the underground water source in the area. The sandstone will change colors from yellow, to red, to pink, and various hues in between as the sun moves from east to west across the sky.

Petra Rediscovered
With the fall of the Roman Empire came a lack of necessary forces to keep law and order in that part of the world. Therefore, the rise of marauding bands and changing trade routes affected the future of the city. In about A.D. 600, Petra again became an isolated city, a home only for vagabonds and wild Arab tradesmen. While it is true that the Crusaders did make an appearance at Petra in the twelfth century, and even built a small castle structure within the city, their influence was inconsequential, and they seemed content to concentrate their efforts far-

ther north at their main castle, Al Karak, adjacent to the Dead Sea.

For over a thousand years Petra remained a ghost town. Those from the outside world who heard of its existence and former glory only half-believed that there ever was such a city. During this time, the Roman Empire fell; the Huns invaded Europe; Columbus discovered America; the Protestant Reformation occurred; European powers established the world colonial system; the Napoleonic wars occurred, as well as the French and American revolutions; and the United States became a nation.

In 1812, John L. Burckhardt, a Swiss adventurer, set out from Cairo, Egypt, determined to find out if the city of Petra was truth or fancy. He had prepared himself by learning Arabic and the basic rituals and beliefs of the Muslim religion. He went first to Syria and turned southward to Philadelphia, which is present-day Amman. He was informed that being a foreigner, he would be killed by the Arabs before he reached his destination. Therefore, he disguised himself as a devout Muslim determined to offer a sacrifice at the tomb of Aaron, which he had heard was on Mount Hor overlooking Petra. No true Muslim could deny a fellow worshipper of Mohammed such a pure and noble goal. Consequently, he was given every aid possible. He was led by a guide down through the Ciq, past the Treasury Building, into the heart of Petra. John Burckhardt's discovery soon led others to this ancient rock city that had been lost in time for one thousand years.

Since 1950, thousands of visitors from all over the world have gone to Petra, the yearly numbers depending upon the political and military situation in the Middle East. However, the city itself, for the most part, remains a ghost town, awaiting patiently its next inhabitants, whom we believe to be a Jewish remnant who will live here for three and a half years, watching for the coming of Messiah.

THE SECRET TREASURE OF SODOM

The name *Petra* is from the Greek, meaning "rock." The Hebrew equivalent is *Sela,* but antedating both names for the Edomite city in the Bible is Mount Seir. *Seir* means "hairy," indicating that God knew in advance that this would be the home of "hairy" Esau.

The first record of Petra in the Bible is found in Genesis 14:1–6:

> And it came to pass in the days of Amraphel king of Shinar, Arioch king of Ellasar, Chedorlaomer king of Elam, and Tidal king of nations; That these made war with Bera king of Sodom, and with Birsha king of Gomorrah, Shinab king of Admah, and Shemeber king of Zeboiim, and the king of Bela, which is Zoar. All these were joined together in the vale of Siddim, which is the salt sea. Twelve years they served Chedorlaomer, and in the thirteenth year they rebelled. And in the fourteenth year came Chedorlaomer, and the kings that were with him, and smote the Rephaims in Ashteroth Karnaim, and the Zuzims in Ham, and the Emims in Shaveh Kiriathaim, And the Horites in their mount Seir, unto Elparan, which is by the wilderness.

We agree with the footnote in the *Pilgrim Bible* which states, in part: "Amraphel. This is another name for the Hammurabi of ancient history." According to the *Encyclopaedia Britannica,* Hammurabi was the sixth king of Babylon who reigned from 2067 B.C. to 2025 B.C.

It is evident that Hammurabi was a contemporary of Abraham. According to *Ussher's Chronology of the Bible,* Abraham lived about 2000 B.C. Hammurabi and an alliance of kings of the countries north of Sodom and Gomorrah overcame an alliance of kings to the south, including Seir. Abraham and an army of 318 men chased the invaders north of Dan to Damascus, where he caught up with them, and rescued Lot and his household. Therefore, Petra was a city in the year 2000 B.C.

In Genesis 11:3, the scripture reveals that the builders of the Tower of Babel used slime as mortar to hold bricks in construction together. Slime, as interpreted by almost any credible Bible dictionary, in biblical usage was bitumen, or asphalt, a semisolid oil residue that seeps to the surface. The Tower of Babel was constructed on the plain of Shinar, or southern Iraq, where today there are vast oil fields.

Crude oil which is pumped out of the ground is a fossil fuel, meaning that it is the decayed residue of animal and plant life. It is evident from the location of the Garden of Eden given in Genesis 2:10–15 that it was located in the general area of what is now Kuwait. There is more oil under the ground of Kuwait than any other place on earth; therefore, this area must have in the distant past been a veritable jungle of both animal and plant life, substantiating the biblical account of the Garden of Eden. Aside from Kuwait, the entire Middle East is a vast reservoir of oil. Much of the oil in the Middle East, including Israel, has not been discovered or developed.

The burning oil fields of Kuwait in the 1991 Desert Storm War, creating an environmental nightmare, were only a warning of more terrible catastrophes to come from burning oil fields in the Middle East:

Come near, ye nations, to hear; and hearken, ye people: let the earth hear . . . and all things that come forth of it. For the indignation of the LORD is upon all nations, and his fury upon all their armies. . . . For it is the day of the LORD's vengeance, and the year of recompences for the controversy of Zion. **And the streams thereof shall be turned into pitch** [oil], and the dust thereof into brimstone, and the land thereof shall become burning pitch. It shall not be quenched night nor day; the smoke thereof shall go up for ever: from generation to generation it shall lie waste; none shall pass through it for ever and ever.

—Isaiah 34:1–2,8–10

God Promises Israel Oil

Israel is practically void of commercial crude oil. There are a few wells along the Mediterranean coastal area, but these are shallow wells and the oil has such high sulphur content that it cannot be used for petroleum conversion. When Israel occupied the Sinai desert, several oil fields were developed. But at the Camp David agreement negotiated by President Jimmy Carter, these oil wells went back to Egypt. However, Egypt was to continue to sell Israel oil until 1992, and this agreement concluded at the end of 1991. Almost one-half of Israel's oil needs had to be compensated for from other sources.

Geological surveys do indicate that there is an abundance of oil in Israel, but at great depths, from 20,000 to 35,000 feet. Hitting the right spot for oil at exactly the right depth is extremely difficult. A friend, Dorsey But-tram, an Oklahoma oilman, related to me that as extensive as the oil fields of Kuwait are, and the vast amount of oil in the ground of Kuwait, fourteen attempts were made before the first oil well was brought in. The problem, of course, is multiplied the deeper the well. An attempt was made by Andrew SoRelle, an oilman from Houston, to hit oil below 20,000 feet in the Haifa area, while drilling in the old land of the tribe of Asher. Mr. SoRelle contends that he did hit an oil pool at 21,000 feet and lost the bit, making impossible the bringing in of the well.

The old land of Asher that extended from what is now the Haifa region northward to Lebanon along the Mediterranean Sea was in the shape of a foot attached to the part of the leg just below the knee. The foot was in the Haifa area, and it is here where serious attempts are being made to bring in the good oil from deep in the earth. Andrew SoRelle relied on the promise of God's blessing upon Asher to verify the geological evidence that there was good oil in that part of Israel: "And of Asher he said, Let Asher be blessed with children; let him be acceptable to his brethren, and let him dip his foot in oil. Thy shoes shall be iron and brass; and as thy days, so shall thy strength be" (Deut. 33:24–25).

Of course, it is a matter of interpretation as to whether God's blessing upon Asher and his descendants referred to olive oil or crude oil. In taking our concordance and tracing all the references to feet in the Bible, we can readily understand just how important this part of the body was to the individual. A person just did not hop in his car, or catch a bus or plane to get from one place to another. The general public did not even own a camel, horse, or donkey. The most common and acceptable method of travel was on foot, and it is evident from Scripture that the feet were washed and anointed quite frequently. It appears that Judas objected to Mary, the sister of Lazarus, using costly ointment to anoint the feet of Jesus rather than using the less expensive olive oil.

To have good feet in excellent physical condition was indeed a blessing in Bible times, but this particular blessing upon Asher could have a double meaning, as many scriptures do, and especially could this be so in light of all the encompassing blessings upon Jacob, his children, and their descendants recorded in the previous chapter:

> For the LORD's portion is his people; Jacob is the lot of his inheritance.... So the LORD alone did lead him, and there was no strange god with him. He made him ride on the high places of the earth, that he might eat the increase of the fields; and he made him to suck honey out of the rock, and **oil out of the flinty rock.**
> —Deuteronomy 32:9,12–13

There is no great mystery about sucking honey out of the rock, because in the Middle East where large hollow trees are scarce, bees often make their hives in rocky cliffs. However, sucking oil out of flinty rock is another matter. If olive oil is meant here, then it could come only by a miracle of God. That God could perform such a miracle is beyond question. However, inasmuch as honey is literally found in the rocks, then within the same context we must look for oil in flinty rocks. As geologists will confirm, crude oil from which petroleum and other fossil fuels are made, is found in flinty rocks, or shale.

We know from Scripture that God's callings and blessings are without repentance. The same applies to His disfavor and wrath. God's blessings upon the three sons of Noah has followed their ordained course, even to this day. Why are God's blessings, callings, and curses without repentance (except in limited qualified circumstances where man himself repents, as with the people at Nineveh)? They are without repentance because God's foreknowledge is absolute. God loved Jacob and hated Esau, even when they were in their mother's womb, committing neither good nor evil. Why? Because God knew what the descendants of Jacob would become and what the descendants of Esau would become. Likewise, the blessings of God upon Jacob and his sons will never be recalled, even if this age and the coming millennial age are required to fulfill them.

Of God's blessings upon Jacob, we read in Genesis 49:24–25:

> But his bow abode in strength, and the arms of his hands were made strong by the hands of the mighty God of Jacob; (from thence is the shepherd, the stone of Israel:) Even by the God of thy father, who shall help thee; and by the Almighty, who shall bless thee with blessings of heaven above, blessings of the deep that lieth under, blessings of the breasts, and of the womb.

We can readily understand God's blessings upon Jacob (which included Israel) in that his descendants have been multiplied, strong in body and spirit. Blessings from Heaven above certainly included the coming of the Great Shepherd, the Rock of Israel, the Lord Jesus Christ. But when we come to "blessings of the deep that lieth under," there is a problem. The deep is not usually associated with blessings unless they could refer to the oil from flinty rocks, as mentioned in Deuteronomy 33. If so, then this blessing has not been manifested, at least not yet.

The Oil of Sodom

It is recorded by Moses in Genesis 10:25 that in the days of Peleg the earth was divided. The word "earth" as used in this verse comes from the Hebrew word meaning "dry land." In other words, at the time of the Tower of Babel, the land mass of the earth began to break up, evidently the result of the breaking up of the fountains of the deep at the time of the great flood. As a result of this "dividing" of the land mass, the continents began to separate and float apart. All this was, of course, according to the will of God in the division of mankind into nations and establishing their boundaries of habitation (Acts 17:26). This massive movement of the earth's land mass naturally frightened the population that had increased since the flood some four hundred years earlier. Moved with fear, they all purposed to build a great tower to keep from being "scattered abroad upon the face of the whole earth" (Gen. 11:4). Geologists and geographers have put all continents and islands back together like a jigsaw puzzle.

Before the destruction of Sodom, Gomorrah, and the nearby towns, the Dead Sea area was a small portion of the earth left over from the pre-flood age: "And Lot lifted up his eyes, and beheld all the plain of Jordan, that it was well watered every where, before the LORD destroyed Sodom and Gomorrah, even as the garden of the LORD, like the land of Egypt, as thou comest unto Zoar" (Gen. 13:10).

The below-sea-level condition with abundant fresh water created a protected hothouse environment. This must have indeed been a beautiful place, but the abomination of mass sexual perversion resulted in the region becoming dead and unhabitable. But there was another problem in beautiful Sodom—slime pits, bitumen surface pools, or seeping oil (Gen. 14:10). These oil bogs evidently figured into the route of the kings of Sodom, Gomorrah, and Edom by the kings of the north led by Amraphel, also known as Hammurabi of Babylon. A few years later, and after Abraham had defeated the kings of the north and saved Lot, God destroyed Sodom and Gomorrah with fire and brimstone in a catastrophic explosion which created the Dead Sea. It has been claimed by many that the mineral and chemical wealth of the Dead Sea is more than the rest of all the world. I have personally always accepted this claim as a zealous exaggeration, although the net worth of the Dead Sea chemicals indeed must be great. But the wealth of the Dead Sea is not due to sedimentary evaporation. Water that comes into the Dead Sea from the Jordan River is good for drinking and irrigation, accounting for 90 percent of Israel's fresh water supply. Under the Dead Sea are salt and chemical deposits hundreds, and possibly thousands, of feet deep.

That there was a Sodom and Gomorrah that was destroyed in a terrible conflagration is beyond question. Josephus wrote in *The Wars of the Jews* that in his time (A.D. 70), the charred remains of the fruit from the trees was still in evidence on the cliffs of the Asphaltic Sea. The Dead Sea was in Josephus' time called the Asphaltic Sea, because it was covered with thick oil which was used to pitch ships. What happened to stop the oil from seeping into the Dead Sea is not known. There was a great earthquake in the eighth century along the African-Syrian Rift that leveled Philadelphia (Amman), Beth Shan, Jerash, and other cities. It is possible that the shifting of the fault line sealed off the oil flow. In any event, as the Bible indicates, the oil is still there. The National Oil Company of Israel, based in Tel Aviv, issued a geological prospectus reporting oil deposits in the Sodom Basin to be in excess of eighteen billion barrels.

The March 16, 1991, edition of the *Jerusalem Post* reported in a front-page article:

Signs of possible reserves have been found in the Negev near the Dead Sea, according to spokesmen of the Israeli National Oil Co. Heavy crude oil, along with natural gas, was discovered at a depth of 3,229 meters [about 10,000 feet] at the INO's East Amiaz One drilling site. Continuous oil samples were reported to be located in a layer of sand thirty meters thick.

One of the problems in drilling so near a fault is that the Syrian plate is shifting to the north, and movement against the African plate could snap lines and bits. It has been predicted by geologists that at some point in time the plates will move to a position where the Valley of Megiddo will open up just south of Haifa and the Mediterranean Sea will pour down the Jordan Valley into the Dead Sea. Such an event would fulfill the prophecy that in the Millennium fish from the Mediterranean Sea will swim in the waters of the Dead Sea (Ezek. 47). Even when this occurs, according to Ezekiel 47:11, the "miry places" (possibly the slime pits) and the "marshes," which are at the southern end in the Sodom Basin, will not be changed. One person who planned to drill in the Sodom Basin was Texas oilman Hayseed Stephens of NESS Energy International of Weatherford, Texas. Mr. Stephens died in 2003.

Some have interpreted Isaiah 60:5, about increasing the wealth of Israel through the converting of the abundance of the sea, to refer to the chemical works at Sodom today. Certainly, this is a source of income to Israel, but tourism and agriculture are the backbone of the economy. If this prophecy refers to the Dead Sea at all, then we would think it would relate to the eighteen billion barrels of oil in the Sodom Basin.

While Sodom has been resurrected from the ashes of history, it remains even today as mainly a few chemical plants and workers' shacks. But let us read what God has in store for Sodom in the future: "When thy sisters, Sodom and her daughters, shall return to their former estate, and Samaria and her daughters shall return to their former estate, then thou and thy daughters shall return to your former estate" (Ezek. 16:55).

Sodom was a city-state, a beautiful place, with a thriving economy, and God says that Sodom will be returned to its former estate. Certainly, an oil boom in the Sodom Basin could bring this to pass.

God has promised Israel in Isaiah 45:3, "And I will give thee the treasures of darkness, and hidden riches of secret places, that thou mayest know that I, the LORD, which call thee by thy name, am the God of Israel."

ESAU HAVE I HATED

B ehind present news regarding both Jordan and Israel is the story of two twins, Jacob, who became the father of Israel, and Esau, who became the father of the Edomite race.

Esau's Blessing

The first place in the Bible where Edom is mentioned is in Genesis 25:24–34:

> And when her days to be delivered were fulfilled, behold, there were twins in her womb. And the first came out red, all over like an hairy garment; and they called his name Esau. And after that came his brother out, and his hand took hold on Esau's heel; and his name was called Jacob: and Isaac was threescore years old when she bare them. And the boys grew: and Esau was a cunning hunter, a man of the field; and Jacob was a plain man, dwelling in tents. And Isaac loved Esau, because he did eat of his venison: but Rebekah loved Jacob. And Jacob sod pottage: and Esau came from the field, and he was faint: And Esau said to Jacob, Feed me, I pray thee, with that same red pottage; for I am faint: therefore was his name called Edom. And Jacob said, Sell me this day thy birthright. And Esau said, Behold, I am at the point to die: and what profit shall this

birthright do to me? And Jacob said, Swear to me this day; and he sware unto him: and he sold his birthright unto Jacob. Then Jacob gave Esau bread and pottage of lentiles; and he did eat and drink, and rose up, and went his way: thus Esau despised his birthright.

Esau had a red complexion, and he sold his birthright for a mess of red beans. Therefore, he was nicknamed Red, or Edom, because *edom* means "red." In the subsequent account, Rebekah induced Jacob to trick Isaac into bestowing the birthright upon him, because Esau had already traded it to him for a bowl of beans. It is evident from the Scriptures that Esau never intended to keep his part of the bargain. The birthright belongs to the eldest son, and Esau had come out of the womb first. In Genesis 27:40–41, we read that the secondary blessing that Isaac bestowed on Esau was that he would live by the sword, that he would have his own dominion, and that he would one day break Jacob's yoke from his neck.

Jacob went north to Haran, and Esau went south to Edom, and we read in Genesis 36:8–9: "Thus dwelt Esau in mount Seir: Esau is Edom. And these are the generations of Esau the father of the Edomites in mount Seir."

God honored Isaac's blessing upon Esau, and gave him the land of Edom. Esau then led his army from Hebron to Petra and killed all the inhabitants, a race of giants. We read of Esau's campaign to take the city in Deuteronomy 2:10–12:

The Emims dwelt therein in times past, a people great, and many, and tall, as the Anakims; Which also were accounted giants, as the Anakims; but the Moabites call them Emims. The Horims also dwelt in Seir beforetime; but the children of Esau succeeded them, when they had destroyed them from before them, and dwelt in their stead; as Israel did unto the land of his possession, which the LORD gave unto them.

To Esau's credit, he dealt with Jacob and his household with loving compassion when it was necessary for Jacob to pass through Esau's territory on the way to Canaan. Jacob was deeply concerned that Esau would kill him and his family and take his cattle and goods. However, we read in Genesis 32–33 that Esau hugged and kissed his brother, gave them safe passage, and even offered to send some of his own men with Jacob to escort them safely to their destination. But otherwise, not much is said to Esau's credit in the Bible.

Esau is not listed among the heroes of the faith in the Old Testament. To the contrary, we read in Hebrews 12:16–17:

Lest there be any fornicator, or profane person, as Esau, who for one morsel of meat sold his birthright. For ye know how that afterward, when he would have inherited the blessing, he was rejected: for he found no place of repentance, though he sought it carefully with tears.

We read in Genesis 25:21 that the birth of Esau and Jacob was an answer to prayer, yet no two brothers could have had such diverse personalities. Esau was a "hale-fellow-well-met." He loved wine, women, and food, and these consumed all of his attention. Jacob, on the other hand, was a "mama's boy," almost an introvert. He planned for the future, and though he often used methods that were less than ethical, he feared God and sought the Lord's will for his life. For these reasons, we read in Malachi 1:2–4:

I have loved you, saith the LORD. Yet ye say, Wherein hast thou loved us? Was not Esau Jacob's brother? saith the LORD: yet I loved Jacob, And I hated Esau, and laid his mountains and his heritage waste for the dragons of the wilderness. Whereas Edom saith, We are impoverished, but we will return and build the desolate places; thus saith the LORD of hosts, They shall build, but I will throw down; and they shall call them, The border of wickedness, and, The people against whom the LORD hath indignation for ever.

In God's foreknowledge, He spoke to Rebekah, ". . . Two nations are in thy womb, and two manner of people shall be separated from thy bowels; and the one people shall be stronger than the other people; and the elder shall serve the younger" (Gen. 25:23).

Esau was born first, but when Jacob came from the womb, he had hold on his brother's heel, indicating that he would indeed supplant the eldest and obtain the birthright and blessings of God. We read also in Hosea 12:3, "He took his brother by the heel in the womb, and by his strength he had power with God."

Paul wrote of Jacob and Esau in Romans 9:11–13 that even from the womb, when neither child had knowledge of, or had done any good or evil, God loved Jacob and hated Esau.

It is difficult for us to comprehend why God would hate one of the twins and love the other, even when both were in a state of innocence as far as awareness of sin is concerned in Rebekah's womb. But God's attitude was not based on what either of the unborn children was or was not, or did or did not do, at the time. God's declaration was made on the basis of His foreknowledge—what Esau would become, what Jacob would become, and how the descendants of each would figure in His eternal plan and purpose. We read in Genesis 25:30 that Esau was called Edom, and in Genesis 32:28 we find, ". . . Thy name shall be called no more Jacob, but Israel. . . ." The nature of Esau, the carnal nature, was thereafter reflected in the national behavior of Edom:

» The Edomites were warlike, preferring to fight their neighbors rather than live in peace (Gen. 27:40).
» The Edomites were idolatrous (2 Chron. 25:14). Esau had a shallow faith and by neither precept nor example did he lead his people to believe in God and seek His will. As a consequence, the Edomites forsook the God of Esau's father, Isaac, and worshipped other gods. On the "high places" in Petra, the sacrificial altars are still preserved. The Edomite priests would take young virgins, burn them on the altars, and then scatter their ashes from the cliffs over the city.
» The Edomites were proud (Jer. 49:16–18). Because they lived in a rock fortress that was easily defended and difficult for outside forces to overcome, they thought they could defy the God of Israel.
» The Edomites were cruel and without mercy toward friend or foe (Jer. 49:19).
» The Edomites were vindictive (Ezek. 25:12). The Edomites never missed an opportunity to torment Israel when Israel was unable to defend itself.

The crimes of Edom against Israel are many:

» When Moses led the children of Israel out of Egypt, the entire company was stranded at Kadesh in the middle of what is now the Negev Desert. The easiest route to the Promised Land from Kadesh was to go east through Petra, northward up the flat mesa on the King's Highway, and then back west down the western slopes of the Gilead Mountains. To have gone straight north from Kadesh would have presented a supply problem, no water, and hostile Canaanite tribes. And so Moses sent the king of Edom the following message: "And Moses sent messengers from Kadesh unto the king of Edom, Thus saith thy brother Israel, Thou knowest all the travail that hath befallen us: How our fathers went down into Egypt, and we have dwelt in Egypt a long time; and the Egyptians vexed us, and our fathers: And when we cried unto the Lord, he heard our voice, and sent an angel, and hath brought us forth out of Egypt: and, behold, we are in Kadesh, a city in the uttermost of thy border: Let us pass, I pray thee, through thy country: we will not pass through the fields, or through the vineyards, neither will we drink of the water of the wells: we will go by the king's high way, we will not turn to the right hand nor to the left, until we have passed thy borders. And Edom said unto him, Thou shalt not pass by me, lest I come out against thee with the sword. And the children of Israel said unto him, We will go by the high way: and if I and my cattle drink of thy water, then I will pay for it: I will only, without doing any thing else, go through on my feet. And he said, Thou shalt not go through. And Edom came out against him with much people, and with a strong hand" (Num. 20:14–20).

As a consequence, Moses had to lead Israel over a torturous route through Ammon. In spite of the fact that Edom and Israel were brother countries, they were turned back and attacked by the Edomite army.

» The Edomites continued to plague Israel, and four hundred years after Moses was refused passage through

Edom, we find that the Edomites and the Israelites were still fighting. In 1 Samuel 14, it is recorded that Saul led Israel against Moab, Ammon, and Edom, and overcame them.

» Two hundred years later, in the reign of Jehoshaphat of Judah, the Moabites, Ammonites, and Edomites again joined in the united effort to utterly destroy every Jew in the land. The combined armies, led by a force from Petra, camped on Mount Olivet with the intention of crossing over the Kidron Valley and attacking Jerusalem. *Jehoshaphat* in the Hebrew means "Jehovah judged." He was the fourth king of Judah after the division of the kingdom into two separate nations. He reigned twenty-five years, between 875 B.C. AND 850 B.C. Jehoshaphat made his share of mistakes, the foremost of which was making an alliance with Ahab, a type of Antichrist. But Jehoshaphat repented, destroyed the groves of the idol worshippers, and sent messengers throughout Judah calling the people to national repentance. A Levite by the name of Jehaziel then informed Jehoshaphat that because he had turned to God for help, the armies of Edom, Ammon, and Moab would be destroyed in the Kidron Valley without the loss of a single man to Israel. The result is recorded in 2 Chronicles 20:23: "...the children of Ammon and Moab stood up against the inhabitants of mount Seir, utterly to slay and destroy them: and when they had made an end of the inhabitants of Seir, every one helped to destroy another."

The prophet Joel referred to the destruction of the enemies of Israel under the leadership of Petra during the reign of Jehoshaphat as a type, or an example, of what will happen at the battle of Armageddon: "Let the heathen be wakened, and come up to the valley of

Jehoshaphat: for there will I sit to judge all the heathen round about. Put ye in the sickle, for the harvest is ripe: come, get you down; for the press is full, the vats overflow; for their wickedness is great. Multitudes, multitudes in the valley of decision: for the day of the LORD is near in the valley of decision" (Joel 3:12–14).

» According to Psalm 137, the inhabitants of Petra and Edom aided Babylon in the destruction of Jerusalem and the Temple, and even begged the Babylonians to level Jerusalem to its foundations so that it would never rise again. And both Jeremiah and Ezekiel indicated that during the Babylonian captivity, the Edomites continually ravaged Judah, robbing the Jews left behind and raping the women. When a remnant was allowed to return and rebuild the walls of the city and the Temple, the Edomites continually threatened the Jews to the extent that they had to work with their armor on and be on guard day and night.

» The Herods were Edomite "stooges" of the Roman government, and Herod the Great killed all the male babies in Israel from two years old and younger. Herod Antipas, who succeeded Herod the Great, beheaded John the Baptist. Pilate sent Jesus Christ to Herod to take jurisdiction over the case that the high priest had brought against Him. It was in this Edomite's power to set Jesus free, but we read in Luke 23:11–12: "And Herod with his men of war set him at nought, and mocked him, and arrayed him in a gorgeous robe, and sent him again to Pilate. And the same day Pilate and Herod were made friends together: for before they were at enmity between themselves."

In mocking Jesus and refusing to accept responsibility, Herod in reality sentenced Jesus to death. Therefore, in looking forward from the time the twins were in the womb of their mother, it is no wonder that God said, "... yet I loved Jacob, And I hated Esau..." (Mal. 1:2–3).

It will be divine justice when God uses this stronghold of Esau, Petra, as a refuge for Israel during the Great Tribulation.

MOSES TO SOLOMON

As we have already noted, Petra was a prominent city from the time of Abraham to the time of Moses. In fact, instead of being ashamed that their historical ancestors treated Moses rather badly, the Arabs in the area have named landmarks after him and his brother Aaron. The spring that flows from a rock formation upon the approach to the Ciq is called Ain Musa, "the spring of Moses." Supposedly, according to local tradition, this is one of the places where Moses struck the rock and water gushed forth. Most Bible commentaries state that Moses brought water out of rock at separate locations, and it is possible one of these was at Petra. It would appear from Scripture that one of the sites was farther to the west.

Regrettably, in 1987 Jordan built an enclosed shelter over Ain Musa to accommodate tourists, but completely blocked off the rock from which the spring flows. Alas, it seems this traditional site of the Mosaic miracle, thirty-five hundred years old, has given way to modern convenience.

Another controversial biblical site that overlooks Petra is Mount Hor. The striking of the rock by Moses to bring forth water, and the death of Aaron on Mount Hor, occurred in the Kadesh-Petra area. Just how near these two events occurred in relation to Petra is in question.

The death of Aaron is recorded in Numbers 20:23–29:

And the LORD spake unto Moses and Aaron in mount Hor, by the coast of the land of Edom, saying, Aaron shall be gathered unto his people: for he shall not enter into the land which I have given unto the children of Israel, because ye rebelled against my word at the water of Meribah. Take Aaron and Eleazar his son, and bring them up unto mount Hor: And strip Aaron of his garments, and put them upon Eleazar his son: and Aaron shall be gathered unto his people, and shall die there. And Moses did as the LORD commanded: and they went up into mount Hor in the sight of all the congregation. And Moses stripped Aaron of his garments, and put them upon Eleazar his son; and Aaron died there in the top of the mount: and Moses and Eleazar came down from the mount. And when all the congregation saw that Aaron was dead, they mourned for Aaron thirty days, even all the house of Israel.

Part of the Petra geological complex is a series of black, jagged mountain peaks. The highest peak is identified as Mount Hor. It is five thousand feet in elevation, the highest of the mountains in the western range that extends from Aqaba to the Dead Sea. Through binoculars, a lightly colored domed shrine can be seen at the very top. The Muslims contend that it is the tomb of Aaron.

In the time of Jesus Christ, Edom was called Idumea. Josephus wrote:

When Moses had made these constitutions, after the sedition was over, he removed, together with the whole army, and came to the borders of Idumea. . . . He caused the army to remove, and to march through the wilderness and through Arabia; and when he came to a place which the Arabians esteem their metropolis, which was formerly called Acre, but has now the name of Petra, at this place, which was encompassed with high mountains, Aaron went up one of them in the sight of the whole army, Moses having before told him that he was to die, for this place was over against them. He put on his pontifical garments, and delivered them to Eleazar his son, to whom the high priesthood belonged, because he was the elder brother; and died while the multitude looked upon him.

—*Antiquities of the Jews,* book 4, chapter 5

Josephus was so called by the Romans. He was a Jewish priest, and his Hebrew name was "Joseph." So it was the accepted belief at the time of Christ that Aaron died on the edge of Petra, on the high mountain that the Arabs today call Mount Hor.

It was for the misstated purpose of offering a sacrifice to the tomb of Aaron that John L. Burckhardt, disguised as a Muslim, gained his entrance to Petra. The Arab name for Mount Hor today is Gebel Haroun. The tomb of Aaron is a holy place to the Muslims, and an "infidel" only attempts a visit to the site at the risk of his life. Because I wanted a picture of the tomb for our annual prophecy calendar, I offered our guide five hundred dollars to take me there. He declined with the excuse that money was no good to a dead man.

However, the following report by G. E. Matson, taken from a story in the February 1935 issue of *National Geographic,* provides us with some information about Aaron's tomb:

More than thirty years ago, when I first visited Petra, the country was quite unsafe. Still, a companion and I ventured with our two Beer-sheba guides up to

the top of Jebel Harun (the mountain of Aaron). The
guides had become very friendly and risked the con-
sequences with us. The going was steep and rocky,
but our ponies carried us almost to the top. We dis-
mounted and scrambled up a knoll, on the summit of
which was a small mosque with a whitewashed dome.
A large antique cistern at the base of this rock showed
us that in ancient times the spot had been much used
by pilgrims (Moslems). Below the shrine, an open natural cave contained three copper cauldrons for seeth-
ing the sacrifice, one so huge as to contain the meat
from a whole camel. Later, as we descended, pilgrims
met us with sheep and goats that they brought here
to kill and eat in fulfillment of a vow. The guides knew
where the key was hidden, and we entered the "Holy of
Holies." Within was built a tomb covered with a dark-
green cloth. This, according to Moslem tradition, is
where Aaron was buried. From the ceiling hung some
eggs of the wild ostriches of the Syrian and North Arabian deserts. We saw on the cenotaph an inscription
in Arabic, as well as one in Hebrew. Built into the ma-
sonry of the north wall, about five feet from the floor,
we saw a black stone of greenish hue that had been
kissed to a shiny surface—a counterpart to the black
stone at Mecca. Both are Dushara. As we prepared to
leave, our guides spied a party of hostile Bedouins
converging on us from afar. A scout had seen the In-
fidels and given the alarm. Hurriedly, but carefully, on
their knees, our men smoothed over every footprint in
the sand that covered part of the floor, as they backed
out to the door. We got halfway down before the Arabs reached the base. They let off a few pot shots, but
our soldier guides called back the wrath of the Turkish
government.

In 1998, a friend from Paris, Texas, went to Petra and did get a guide to take him to Aaron's tomb. He said it was a full day's effort. He shared with me some of the pictures taken, and one is included in the picture section of this book. We were fortunate to obtain a picture of this biblical and historic site that few Christians or Jews have witnessed.

Josephus called Petra a city in the Arabian wilderness, and he reported the consensus of Jewish interpretation concerning the journey of Moses to the Promised Land; i.e., that Moses and all of Israel came from Kadesh to the entrance of Petra, and there messengers were sent to speak to the king. The Josephus report lends credibility to the belief by the Muslims that the spring, Ain Musa, is one of the spots where Moses brought water out of the rock, and that the high imposing mountain overlooking Petra is Mount Hor.

According to Deuteronomy 1:44–46, Moses and the children of Israel were in Petra,

> And the Amorites, which dwelt in that mountain, came out against you, and chased you, as bees do, and destroyed you in Seir, even unto Hormah. And ye returned and wept before the LORD; but the LORD would not hearken to your voice, nor give ear unto you. So ye abode in Kadesh many days, according unto the days that ye abode there.

The first four verses of the second chapter of Deuteronomy state that Moses and the congregation stayed at Petra for many days because the "children of Esau" would not let them pass through.

As far as the location of Mount Hor is concerned, we read in Genesis 14:6 that the Horites lived in Mount Seir, and here again the Scriptures lend support to the Arab tradition that Mount Hor is the high mountain at Petra, the place of Aaron's death.

Another interesting scripture that sheds light on the relation of Petra to Israel's wanderings in the wilderness is Deuteronomy 33:1–2:

> And this is the blessing, wherewith Moses the man of God blessed the children of Israel before his death. And he said, The LORD came from Sinai, and rose up from Seir unto them; he shined forth from mount Paran, and he came with ten thousands of saints: from his right hand went a fiery law for them.

The three main places that God showed His power and glory to Israel, after the crossing of the Red Sea, were at Mount Sinai, Mount Seir, and Mount Paran. Mount Seir refers to Petra and Mount Paran to the general Kadesh area.

Petra During David's Reign

During the reign of the judges, from about 1400 B.C. to 1000 B.C., the Israelites lived through periods of grace and prosperity and periods of war and famine. It would seem that the twelve tribes were occupied for much of this era with establishing homes, cultivating the land, and either trying to make friends with, or exterminate if the need arose, their neighbors: the Philistines, Canaanites, Ammonites, Moabites, and the other various peoples in Israel, Lebanon, Syria, Ammon, and Moab. Being on the southern edge of Israel and somewhat removed by a wild, desert, and mountainous area, the Edomites were not threatened by Israel at that time because Israel was too busy dealing with problems nearer home. Therefore, the Edomites seemed content with sending small raiding parties to rob and pillage isolated villages and outposts. Of this period, and leading up to the reign of Israel's second king, David, we quote from the book *Petra* by Iain Browning:

Perhaps it was during the exodus the Edomite "king," Rekem, refused the wanderers passage through his lands, necessitating a vast detour before they could reach their Promised Land. And yet the future King David went to a friendly Edom to hide from the fury of King Saul.

However, when David eventually became king in about 1000 B.C., he promptly attacked Moab and Edom and subdued them, exterminating two-thirds of the former and leaving his general, Joab, to massacre every male Edomite he could find. Admittedly, the Edomites had been raiding Palestine on a regular basis for a very long time. . . . A Song of Triumph seems to have been in order on such occasions, and King David did himself proud of this particular one if the sixtieth psalm is anything to go by. . . . The whole history of the Edomites after this appears to be a continual state of hostility with the Hebrews—particularly Judah. They suffered from a succession of disastrous confederacies with their northern neighbors Moab and Ammon—or both—all of which were ruthlessly smashed by their oppressors. It came to such a point that during the reign of Solomon, the people of Edom were not enslaved as they had been in the reign of David. It is probable that during the previous reign, the population of Edom had been so savagely depleted that it was necessary to release them to prevent the land from going out of cultivation altogether and returning to the desert.

There were moments when Edom regained her independence for a short while, but this required that they wage a ferocious and relenting war against Judeans in order to keep it. . . . The almost constant massacres they seem to have suffered lead one to wonder where their forces came from: each time there was a battle, it was recorded that the people of Edom were virtually exterminated."

God's pronouncement of judgment against Seir and Edom was that although they would be built up, they would be torn down. If they were built up again, God would tear them down again.

As previously noted, Petra was a place of refuge for David when King Saul gave orders to kill him. But it was not out of love for David that the Edomites befriended him. King Saul invaded Edom and Israel's army successfully carried out a murderous campaign against the Edomites. Therefore, as with political refugees today, any enemy of Saul was a friend of Edom.

The apostle Paul in Galatians 1:7 stated that after his conversion, when he was let down over the walls of Damascus to escape the Jews, he went to Arabia for a period of three years. Petra was then the capital city of Arabia, as noted by Josephus and others. One of the two main trade routes through Petra went north to Damascus. It is probable that Paul was a refugee in Petra for three years. He would have been received warmly for the same reason that David was received kindly by the Edomites.

However, when David became king of Israel, he went to war against Edom. The account is given in 2 Samuel 8:11–14:

Which also king David did dedicate unto the LORD,

with the silver and gold that he had dedicated of all
nations which he subdued; Of Syria, and of Moab, and
of the children of Ammon, and of the Philistines, and
of Amalek, and of the spoil of Hadadezer, son of Rehob,
king of Zobah. And David gat him a name when he returned from smiting of the Syrians in the valley of salt,
being eighteen thousand men. And he put garrisons in
Edom; throughout all Edom put he garrisons, and all
they of Edom became David's servants. And the LORD
preserved David whithersoever he went.

When the army of Israel was engaged in a war with another nation, or Israel was invaded by outside armies, the
Edomites always seized the opportunity to attack Jewish
settlements near the border with Edom. David and his
army engaged in a war with Syria, and the king of Edom
with his army invaded Israel. The armies of Edom and
Israel met in combat in the Valley of Salt, identified tra-
ditionally as a five-mile stretch of salt-covered ground to
the south of the Dead Sea. It might be interpreted that David killed eighteen thousand Syrians, but 2 Samuel 8:13
really means that these were Edomites, because the Syrians would not have been that far south. Afterward, Edom
became occupied land during David's reign, controlled
by garrisons of Israeli soldiers stationed throughout the
nation. It would appear obvious that the main occupying
force would have been stationed at Petra. Verse fourteen
states that "Edom became David's servants," again fulfilling the prophecy that the elder twin, Esau, would serve
the younger, Jacob.

Petra During Solomon's Reign
One of Esau's earliest mistakes was in his choice of wom-

en. We quote from *The Sarcophagus of an Ancient Civilization:*

> Esau married Hittite wives—Judith and Bashemath (Gen. 26:34). This was another blunder. They were heathen and therefore beneath him. Heathenism has never produced a very exalted type of womanhood. Rebekah was sorely tried by these "daughters of Heth." Yet his marriage promoted by no passionate impulse of the moment any more than was the sale of his birthright. In his rovings he had associated freely with the Hittites, though he knew that they were "strangers to the covenant of promise," eating and drinking, sacrificing, and eventually vowing with them. His ideals were low. A man's choice in his marriage, more than anything else in his life, makes it manifest what that man is, and where his heart it.

Solomon made the same mistake. We read in 1 Kings 11:1–4:

> But king Solomon loved many strange women, together with the daughter of Pharaoh, women of the Moabites, Ammonites, Edomites, Zidonians, and Hittites; Of the nations concerning which the LORD said unto the children of Israel, Ye shall not go in to them, neither shall they come in unto you: for surely they will turn away your heart after their gods: Solomon clave unto these in love. And he had seven hundred wives, princesses, and three hundred concubines: and his wives turned away his heart. For it came to pass, when Solomon was old, that his wives turned away his heart after other gods....

Of all the foreign wives and concubines that Solomon took, none were more dangerous than the Edomite women. The Edomites were Israel's most bitter enemy, and Solomon worshipped the false gods of Mount Seir. Nevertheless, Edom was an important part of the kingdom of Israel under Solomon. We read in 2 Chronicles 8:17, "Then went Solomon to Eziongeber, and to Eloth, at the sea side in the land of Edom."

Although there may be some disagreement as to the original sites of Ezion-geber and Eloth, it is generally conceded that Eloth is modern Eilat and Ezion-geber is possibly Aqaba. Both cities are on the Gulf of Aqaba, a narrow bay off the Red Sea. Eilat is in Israel and Aqaba is in Jordan, about five miles apart and clearly in view of each other across the bay.

Cool, moist air pours down the Jezreel Valley from the Mediterranean Sea to the Sea of Galilee area, six hundred feet below sea level, and continues southward down the Jordan Valley to the Dead Sea, thirteen hundred feet below sea level. During the day, the air is heated. Pressure cooker-type results send winds down the Arabah. The winds shear off up the canyons on either side in sheets of about ten feet high. Egyptian engineers captured these winds in blast furnaces where ore was heated to a degree high enough to extract the metal. At Timna, ten miles north of Eilat, these furnaces are still much in evidence, and copper slag still covers the ground. Mushroom rock formations in the area attest to the velocity and depth of these winds.

Moses doubtless was well informed about the area before he led the children of Israel through this region. Later, Solomon must have used these mines and furnaces to obtain metal for his chariots and building purposes. It is recorded in 2 Chronicles 8–9 that Solomon built up his navy at Ezion-geber, and through this port came gold, precious stones, spices, and merchandise of many kinds from Sheba, Ethiopia, and as far away as China.

Solomon built the House of God, fortifications at Megiddo, a navy, and initiated building projects in Jerusalem and many other cities in Israel. He is depicted in the Bible as perhaps the richest man in the world of his day. Most of this wealth came through Petra, a valuable trade center even in 1000 B.C. This was why it was important for Solomon to have control of the red rock city, but he chose the wrong way to do it by marrying idolatrous Edomite wives.

Although the Edomites were robbers and murderers, during the reign of Solomon it would have been fairly safe for traders and merchants to ship their wares through this region. Petra was an ideal way-station, providing shelter, water, and food. One of the more notable travelers to have passed through Petra would have been the Queen of Sheba, as the main highway from her country to Jerusalem went through the city. We can almost see this majestic queen on the lead camel passing through El Ciq.

In 2 Chronicles 9:1-12 is found a rather lengthy account of the Queen of Sheba's (or Seba) visit to see if all she had heard about the wealth and wisdom of the handsome king of Israel, Solomon, was true. From the biblical account, it is evident that the queen was exceedingly impressed, so much so that she declared that Solomon was actually double all that she had heard about him. She gave Solomon gold, spices, and precious stones, and Solomon gave her "... all her desire, whatsoever she asked...."

The Bible does not say how long the Queen of Sheba stayed in Israel in "communion" with Solomon. It could have been a week, a month, a year, or longer. In any event, according to both Jewish and Ethiopian tradition, the queen gave birth to a son by Solomon. The boy's name was, according to the Ethiopian royal chronicles, Menelik I. The Jewish population of Ethiopia is commonly accepted as being descendants of the male offspring of Solomon and the ancient queen. The government of Israel accepts this traditional story as being true; thus, Operation Solomon was initiated in 1991 to finally bring home these long-lost Jewish brethren to await the coming of Messiah.

The ancient traditional records, accepted as literal history by many, also relate that Menelik remained with Solomon, was educated in Jerusalem, and taught the writings of Moses and the Jewish religion.

Grant Jeffrey, in his book *Armageddon: Appointment with Destiny,* provides the following related information:

> In a September 1935 article in the *National Geographic* magazine, L. Roberts recorded his interviews with various priests in different parts of Ethiopia who consistently told the same story. They recounted that the Queen of Sheba had visited King Solomon and had "a child, Menelik I. Solomon educated the lad in Jerusalem until he was nineteen years old. The boy then returned to Ethiopia with a large group of Jews, taking with him the true Ark of the Covenant." Many people believe that this Ark is now in some church along the northern boundary of present-day Ethiopia, near Aduwa or Aksum; but, if it is here, it is so well guarded by priests that no student from the Western world has been able to confirm or deny the legend. The *Encyclopaedia Britannica* confirms this tradition: [Aksum-Aduwa] contains the ancient church where, according to tradition, the Tabot, or Ark of the Covenant, brought from Jerusalem by the son of Solomon and the Queen of Sheba, was deposited and is still supposed to rest.

The traditional story affirms that before Menelik returned to his mother in Ethiopia at the age of nineteen, Solomon had prepared for him an exact replica of the Ark of the Covenant. However, Menelik switched the duplicate for the real thing and took it with him. Solomon, according to the extra-biblical story, had been corrupted by his foreign wives and had even allowed idols in the Temple. So, possibly in conspiracy with the high priest, Menelik took the artifact, hoping to return it when true worship of God returned to Israel. A report in the *B'nai B'rith Messenger* (a Jewish publication) reported in 1935 that the Tablets of the Law received by Moses on Mount Sinai and the Ark of the Covenant, taken to Ethiopia by Menelik, had been taken to Abyssinia during the Italian invasion for safekeeping. There are other sources we could quote that would seem to add credibility to this rather common belief among the Falasha Jews that the real Ark is in Ethiopia.

Prior to the visit of the Queen of Sheba, the "ark of the Lord" is mentioned as being in the Temple built by Solomon (2 Chron. 8:11). It is indeed remarkable that before 2 Chronicles 8:11, the Ark of the Covenant is mentioned approximately two hundred times, but afterward in the Old Testament, it is mentioned only twice, and one of these two times (Jer. 3:16) is a millennial reference. In the days of Josiah there was mention of the Ark (2 Chron. 35:3), but it could be argued that this was the duplicate ark. It is apparent that after 2 Chronicles 8:11 (1000 B.C.), the Ark evidently did not fill a prominent place in the religious life of Israel. Whether this was because the real Ark was gone or not is debatable.

While most of the sacred vessels of the Temple were taken to Babylon by Nebuchadnezzar, nothing is reported about the Ark during the Babylonian captivity, or the returning of the Ark by the priesthood. The Maccabees in about 170 B.C. did report, according to their information, that Jeremiah hid the Ark in a cave in Mount Nebo just before the Temple was destroyed by the Babylonians (2 Macb. 2:4–8). Tom Crotser of Kansas claimed to have found the Ark under the old Byzantine church on Mount Nebo, but his claim is completely discounted by the government of Jordan. There is no reason for Jordan to deny the report if it were true, as the Ark of the Covenant in Jordan would mean millions in tourist dollars.

There are other nebulous rumors that the zealots carried the Ark with them to Masada before the Romans laid siege to Jerusalem in A.D. 70, or that the Romans took the Ark to Rome after the destruction of the Temple and that it is now hidden in the basement of St. Peter's Cathedral. Yet the most consistent and supportive tradition concerning the mystery of the disappearance of the Ark is that it has been hidden in Ethiopia. We do not say this is true, or not true; but if such can even possibly be the case, then the Falasha Jews would certainly have brought the Ark with them, or made plans to have it brought to them later.

In Isaiah 18 we read of a description of Ethiopia, which could well apply to that famine-ridden and troubled land today. In verse seven we read, "In that time shall the present be brought unto the Lord of hosts. . . ." The footnote in my *Pilgrim Bible* reads, "The present is the people of Israel . . . but who will return. . . ." The black Jews of Ethiopia have moved to Israel, but the promise of bringing a "present" may have a double meaning. The Hebrew word for "present," or "gift" is *nes*, interpreted "ark" by some scholars.

The late emperor Haile Selassie of Ethiopia claimed to be of the royal line of Solomon through Menelik and bore the title, "Lion of the Tribe of Judah." The royal line from Solomon through Menelik has been maintained for three thousand years. After the communist coup in 1975, most of the royal family have been residing in Canada. Whether they will rejoin their countrymen in Israel is not known at this time.

Falasha means "stranger," and the black Jews in Ethiopia upon returning to Israel in "eagle wings," as prophesied, have expressed feelings that after three thousand years they have finally come home.

On the weekend of May 25, 1991, in a span of just 36 hours, 14,500 black Ethiopian Jews were airlifted from Addis Ababa to Tel Aviv. Television cameras at Ben Gurion airport relayed the amazing scene of Jews in Israel greeting their black brethren with hugs, kisses, food, and clothing. In Israel, the black Jews from the south were hailed as another important sign that the messianic age was dawning upon the land of the Bible.

The return of a remnant of Israel from the nations of the world before the "great and terrible day of the Lord" is prophesied in many places in the Bible. However, the exact order of the return is given in Isaiah 43:4–6:

> Since thou wast precious in my sight, thou hast been honourable, and I have loved thee: therefore will I give men for thee, and people for thy life. Fear not: for I am with thee: I will bring thy seed from the east, and gather thee from the west; I will say to the north, Give up; and to the south, Keep not back: bring my sons from far, and my daughters from the ends of the earth.

In Beijing, on one of my visits to that city, I was startled to read about Jews in China (Sinim) who looked like Chinese, dressed like Chinese, ate and lived like Chinese, yet who kept the Sabbath and the law of Moses. After the Communist victory in China and the subsequent massacre of 60 million, many Chinese Jews returned to Israel in the midst of a slaughter of humanity. From the east (which includes the Middle East) thousands have returned from the Arab nations.

After World War II, the bloodiest war ever to shake the earth, Jews returned from the Western European nations. Then, for several decades it appeared that the Jews in the north (Russia) would not be allowed to return (could the Bible be wrong?). But then, with threatened internal revolution and famine, Russia suddenly allowed Jews to go through Helsinki and return to Israel, their homeland. One dear little lady in Helsinki who listens to the Southwest Radio Church is a friend of the prime minister of Finland. She took him some of our literature and warned him that if he did not allow the Jews to go through his country, he would be cursed of God. A million Jews have now immigrated to Israel from Russia, and thousands are returning every month.

According to Isaiah, the Jews would return first from the east, then the west, then the north, and finally, the south. In 1985 a secret deal was made with the Communist government of Ethiopia to ransom the black Jews in Ethiopia to the Israelis. The order of the returning remnant is complete as given by the prophet Isaiah. No other Jews have to return in order to fulfill the prophecies relating to the regathering before the Great Tribulation.

SOLOMON
TO THE NABATEANS

As God had foretold concerning the Edomites, the descendants of Esau were distrusted and often despised by neighboring nations. Even when they were allied with the Ammonites and Moabites for common defense, their allies had rather fight them than the enemy. What happened at the Kidron Valley in the reign of Jehoshaphat is a case in point.

We read in 1 Samuel 22 that Saul had an Edomite servant by the name of Doeg. At that time there was a village outside of Jerusalem called Nob. Nob was the home of eighty-five priests, their families, and a few hundred other local residents. David passed through Nob, and the priests, being uninformed about the controversy that David had with Saul, gave David food. The biblical account of what followed is recorded in 1 Samuel 22:9–10,18–19:

> Then answered Doeg the Edomite, which was set over
> the servants of Saul, and said, I saw the son of Jesse
> coming to Nob, to Ahimelech the son of Ahitub. And
> he enquired of the Lord for him, and gave him victuals,
> and gave him the sword of Goliath the Philistine. . . .
> And the king said to Doeg, Turn thou, and fall upon the
> priests. And Doeg the Edomite turned, and he fell upon

the priests, and slew on that day fourscore and five persons that did wear a linen ephod. And Nob, the city of the priests, smote he with the edge of the sword, both men and women, children and sucklings, and oxen, and asses, and sheep, with the edge of the sword.

Psalm 52, a psalm of David, appears to be his lament that the servants of the Lord who had helped him were so cruelly slain by an evil man. Afterward, when David's army killed eighteen thousand Edomites in the Valley of Salt, he purposed to put an end to the Edomites as a race of people, and we read of this effort at genocide that almost succeeded in 1 Kings 11:14–19,24–25:

And the LORD stirred up an adversary unto Solomon, Hadad the Edomite: he was of the king's seed in Edom. For it came to pass, when David was in Edom, and Joab the captain of the host was gone up to bury the slain, after he had smitten every male in Edom; (For six months did Joab remain there with all Israel, until he had cut off every male in Edom:) That Hadad fled, he and certain Edomites of his father's servants with him, to go into Egypt; Hadad being yet a little child. And they arose out of Midian, and came to Paran: and they took men with them out of Paran, and they came to Egypt, unto Pharaoh king of Egypt; which gave him an house, and appointed him victuals, and gave him land. And Hadad found great favour in the sight of Pharaoh, so that he gave him to wife the sister of his own wife, the sister of Tahpenes the queen. . . . And he gathered men unto him, and became captain over a band, when David slew them of Zobah: and they went to Damascus, and dwelt therein, and reigned in Damascus. And he was an adversary to Israel all the days of Solomon, beside the mischief that Hadad did: and he abhorred Israel, and reigned over Syria.

We read in the same chapter that Solomon had married Edomite wives and they had led him into worshipping the false gods of Edom, and God was angry with Solomon. The Edomite prince Hadad had escaped from Joab when he attempted to kill every Edomite male according to David's instructions. Therefore, the Lord stirred up Hadad against Solomon, and He placed this Edomite in a strong position in Syria. He was a thorn to Solomon all the days of his reign. In this instance, God used an Edomite to punish Israel for the transgressions of Solomon.

After Solomon, Israel was divided into separate states. In 940 b.c., the ten tribes of the northern kingdom, Israel, made Jereboam king, and the southern kingdom, composed of two tribes (Benjamin and Judah), made Rehoboam king. The male population had been decimated by David, and although the Edomites tried repeatedly to regain their independence, they were unsuccessful. We read in 1 Kings 22:47 that there was no king in Edom, but a deputy appointed by Judah governed the land. It was in this period that the Edomites joined with Ammon and Moab to attack Jerusalem when Jehoshaphat was king, but were again annihilated. Jehoshaphat subsequently attempted to rebuild the navy at Ezion-geber, but his ships were sunk. Whether this disaster was due to a storm, or a revolt of the Edomites, is unclear.

The Edomites rebelled again during the reign of Jehoram, and although he and his army escaped from an ambush, Edom gained a measure of independence (2 Kings 8; 2 Chron. 21:8–10). In 839 b.c., the Edomites had regained sufficient strength to again invade Israel, but we read in 2 Kings 14:7 that Amaziah, the fourth king of Judah, ". . . slew of Edom in the valley of salt ten thousand, and took Selah by war. . . ." After Amaziah conquered Petra, he threw another ten thousand Edomites from the cliffs: "And other ten thousand left alive did the children of Judah carry away captive, and brought them unto the top of the rock, and cast them down from the top of the rock, that they all were broken in pieces" (2 Chron. 25:12).

All who have been to Petra can imagine the awesome scene as ten thousand Edomites were taken to the top of the five hundred foot cliffs and thrown down to the stone boulders below. This was supposed to have been a gruesome object lesson to the Edomites to never invade Israel again.

However, Amaziah in the aftermath of victory, was so impressed with the high places in Petra that he set up altars to the gods of Edom in Israel and worshipped them. For this, he suffered judgment from the Lord and he was subsequently slain at Lachish (2 Chron. 25).

About forty years later, the Edomites were up to their old tricks. Amos wrote his prophecy in the days of Uzziah, king of Judah, about 787 B.C., and we read in the first chapter of Amos that they purchased Hebrew slaves from the Philistines and Tyre, doubtless for resale to the merchant caravans that passed through Petra. For this reason, the prophet wrote in Amos 1:9 that God would not spare Edom, because they remembered not the "brotherly covenant," and this pronouncement is found in verse eleven: "Thus saith the Lord; For three transgressions of Edom, and for four, I will not turn away the punishment thereof; because he did pursue his brother with the sword, and did cast off all pity, and his anger did tear perpetually, and he kept his wrath for ever."

The brotherly covenant is given in Deuteronomy 23:7:

"Thou shalt not abhor an Edomite; for he is thy brother...." God declared that this covenant was set aside because of the continual anger at Edom against Israel, and the scripture indicates that it was the Edomites who first tried to kill their brothers, the Israelites, with the sword. The Edomites were not selective in slave traffic, and it would appear they also sold Moabites into slavery. The Moabites subsequently took Petra and burned the bones of their former kings into ash. We went into one of the cave dwellings that was used for tombs for royalty, and there are no bones in the ancient sepulchres (Amos 2:1–2).

For another forty years Judah continued to hold the Eilat area to the south of Petra, but the hold was completely broken in the days of Ahaz, king of Israel, and according to prophecy, will not be restored until the last half of the Tribulation. We read in 2 Kings 16:6 (written in 739 B.C.): "At that time Rezin king of Syria recovered Elath to Syria . . . and dwelt there unto this day."

Assyria was a rising power to the east, and Shabaska of the twenty-fifth dynasty in Egypt sent an undercover agent to Edom to foment a rebellion against the new empire. He feared that Assyria would extend its control to Egypt, and he promised the Edomites that aid would be forthcoming in the event of war. The year was 715 B.C. Shabaska even promised the northern kingdom, Israel, and the southern kingdom, Judah, help if they would stand up to the Assyrians. Egypt, even at that time, had a record of failing to live up to such treaties, and this doubtless prompted the warning to Isaiah:

Woe to them that go down to Egypt for help; and stay on horses, and trust in chariots, because they are many; and in horsemen, because they are very strong;

but they look not unto the Holy One of Israel, neither seek the LORD!... Now the Egyptians are men, and not God; and their horses flesh, and not spirit. When the LORD shall stretch out his hand, both he that helpeth shall fall, and he that is holpen shall fall down, and they all shall fail together.

—Isaiah 31:1,3

The Edomites did rebel against Assyria, and subsequently Sargon II led a campaign into Edom against Petra. The Edomites who escaped fled to Samaria and settled in northern Palestine, providing initial evidence that the Palestinians of today are of partial Edomite ancestry. Thus, the enmity between Esau and Jacob continues to this day, even as God said it would.

Sargon conquered Israel and the ten tribes of Samaria were taken into captivity. In 705 B.C., Sennacherib became king of Assyria, and shortly thereafter invaded Judah. Jerusalem was besieged, but God intervened and in one night 85,000 Assyrians in Sennacherib's army died (2 Kings 19:35–37). The remainder of the Assyrian army withdrew to Nineveh and Judah was spared.

One hundred years later, Nebuchadnezzar of Babylon threatened Judah with an invasion. The king of Edom enticed Zedekiah into entering a military alliance against Babylon for the purpose of mutual defense, and according to Jeremiah 40, when Nebuchadnezzar marched against Jerusalem, many of the Jews fled to Edom and Petra for safety. But when Jerusalem fell, the Edomites rejoiced. We read in Lamentations 4:21–22:

Rejoice and be glad, O daughter of Edom, that dwellest in the land of Uz; the cup also shall pass through unto thee: thou shalt be drunken, and shalt make thyself naked. The punishment of thine iniquity is accomplished, O daughter of Zion; he will no more carry thee away into captivity: he will visit thine iniquity, O daughter of Edom; he will discover thy sins.

The futility of Judah's alliance with Edom is also reflected in Psalm 137:1,7: "By the rivers of Babylon, there we sat down, yea, we wept, when we remembered Zion. . . . Remember, O LORD, the children of Edom in the day of Jerusalem; who said, Rase it, rase it, even to the foundation thereof."
The Edomites became willing vassals of Babylon. During the Babylonian captivity, they occupied the land in the Hebron-Beersheba area. This note provides further evidence that the Palestinian Arabs are of Edomite extraction. Those who took up residence in Israel became known as Idumeans (*History of Babylonia and Assyria* by R. W. Rogers). The Edomites seemed to prefer the more fertile land in Israel to barren and rock-bound Petra, and for the most part, deserted their former homeland. It was at this time that Petra became inhabited by a race of people called the Nabateans. Quoting from *The Sarcophagus of an Ancient Civilization:*

It is not possible to determine exactly when they [the Nabateans] occupied the Edomite territory of Seir and made Petra their chief stronghold, but it is highly probable that it was in the sixth century B.C. For, when the Jews were taken to Babylon, the Edomites pushed north to occupy their territory, and it would have been easy then for the Nabateans in turn to take part of the Edomite territory.

The Nabateans

The Nabateans occupied Petra until it lapsed into obscurity. It was under their administration that Petra reached the height of its glory as an important trade center. But few ancient historians would agree as to just who the Nabateans were or where they came from. Josephus, reflecting the common Jewish belief of his day, wrote that they were descendants of Nebajoth, the firstborn of Ishmael. Diodorus Siculus, writing in the year 60 B.C., simply referred to them as Arabs. He observed that in some ways they were like the Syrians, but in other ways, the Arabians. We quote from Siculus' dissertation:

> The Nabateans: They water their cattle every three days, lest while fleeing in waterless places they should require to be watered every day. Their own food is meat and milk and such edible things as spring from the ground. Pepper grows among them, and much of what is called wild honey comes from the trees which they use mixed with water as a drink. There are also other races of Arabs, some of whom till the ground . . . and some features in common with the Syrians, except the living in houses. These, then, are found to be the manners and customs of the Arabians; and there being near to them a great fair held to which the neighbors were wont to resort, some to sell their wares, others to buy anything they had use for, they journeyed to this, leaving in a rock their possessions, and their oldest men, along with the children and wives.

Strabo, who lived between 66 B.C. and A.D. 24, said, "The Idumeans are Nabateans." This statement would indicate that he believed them to be nothing more than a resurgence of the Edomite race. However, according to Strabo's own writings, the Nabateans were as different from the Edomites as night is from day. His own description of the Nabateans states that they were a friendly, yet fiercely liberty-loving and independent people. We quote Strabo:

> The capital of the Nabateans is called Petra ... which is externally abrupt and precipitous, but within there are abundant springs of water both for domestic purposes and for watering gardens. . . . Athenodorus, a philosopher and my friend, who had visited Petra, used to relate with surprise, that he found many Romans and also many other strangers residing there; that the strangers frequently engaged in litigation, both with one another and with the natives; but that the natives had never had any dispute amongst themselves, and lived together in perfect harmony. The Nabateans are prudent, and fond of accumulating property. The community fines a person who has diminished his substance, and they confer honors on him who has increased it. They have few slaves, and are served for the most part by their relations, or by one another ... and this custom extends even to their kings. They eat their meals in companies consisting of thirteen. Each company is attended by two musicians. . . . No one drinks more than eleven cupfuls, from separate cups, each of gold. The king is so democratic that in addition to serving himself, he sometimes even ministers to others. He often submits his public accounts to the people, and sometimes also the conduct of his life is inquired into. Their houses are sumptuous, and of stone. . . . They look upon the bodies of the dead as no better than dung. . . . Wherefore they even bury their kings beside dung heaps. They worship the sun, and construct the altar on the top of the house, pouring out libations and

burning frankincense upon it every day.

On my November 2008 tour to Israel, which also included Petra, I made it a special issue to ask natives in the Petra area, including the young men in charge of the horses and buggies, about their tribal and/or racial background. Without exception, everyone said they were Nabateans, descendants of Ishmael. All protested they were not Edomites or Palestinians.

Other historical sources alternately identify the Nabateans as Armenians, Chaldeans, Ishmaelites, and Edomites. Regardless, it was under the Nabatean administration in Petra that huge water cisterns were built, cave dwellings that would hold up to three thousand people were carved out of the sandstone, and general water systems were improved. All these improvements are still in evidence today and will be used by the Jews when they occupy Petra during the last half of the Tribulation.

THE RELIGION
OF PETRA

As noted in the *National Geographic* magazine of February 1933, there are more than one thousand monuments and temples in Petra. The majority of these structures were of Nabatean identity; however, some were constructed during Edomite times, a few are of Roman design, a few were used by early Christians, and there are even the remains of a Crusader castle.

Little is known about the religion of the Horites, the earliest settlers of Petra. Esau, the father of the Edomites, was a sensual and profane person, displaying little standards of ethics of any religion. Nevertheless, the Edomites must have obtained a deep conviction concerning respect for the dead and a belief in the afterlife. Such is evidenced by the elaborate tombs that filled the metropolis. Inasmuch as the Nabateans had no respect for the bodies of the dead, the tombs must have been the work of the Edomites. The vengeful deed of the Moabites in burning the bones of the Edomite dead seems to verify this point (Amos 2:1).

Esau spurned his birthright and embraced no commitment to the covenants and promises God made to Abraham, Isaac, and Jacob. There was no repentance by Esau, and his acknowledgment of any god would have to be to one other than the God of his fathers. It is recorded in 2 Chronicles 20 that during the days of King Joash, Israel worshipped false gods of Edom. The chief Edomite god seems to have been Kaush, represented by the Egyptian scarab. The veneration of the patriarchs and the prophets by the Arab world did not emerge until A.D. 600 with Mohammed. It has been commonly reported that the Koran itself was the work of a Nestorian Christian and an apostate Jew.

Venus, also called Ishtar, was the goddess of the morning star. She was worshipped by the Nabateans under the name Al Uzza. Dusares, another Nabatean deity, was called a "good god." The chief place of worship in Petra was the high place overlooking the city. This place of sacrifice is well preserved and consists of a high altar, a nearby round altar (possibly for small animal offerings), the offering table where the sacrifice was killed, the drainage channel, and the water basin for cleansing. It appears obvious that both the Edomites and Nabateans practiced sacrificial worship, as was the case with almost all races and nations of the world during that age. From the book *Petra* by Browning, we read the author's own interpretation of the blood sacrifice:

> The nature of blood sacrifice, indeed sacrifice of any kind, is probably very different from what the majority of people today think. Popular fiction has always presented it as a kind of barbaric practice attended by brutal pagan rites. The painful and unpleasant sides, the element of denial, have always been stressed, as has the loss of life of the victim, the ultimate denial, so that sacrifice becomes a payment by suffering. Even the use of the word "victim" implies suffering. Yet in ancient times, when symbolism was understood by even

the most uneducated, sacrifice engendered feelings of joy and happiness at the working of Grace. It was seen as a renewal of the close relationship between man and deity, a sort of mystical union with God. Blood, in popular terms, is the symbol of suffering, but in ancient times it was the symbol of life, indeed, was the source of life. By the use of blood in the ritual sacrifice, the congregation expected a renewal of life and divine protection, but because blood was the sole property of God, certain uses, such as drinking it, were taboo. But by having blood ritually sprinkled on his family, his house, or his goods, a man would be invoking the deity for a continuance of his prosperity.

According to the biblical meaning of a blood sacrifice as commanded by God to the Hebrews, it signified payment for sin, or redemption from sin. Only animals or fowls were used in sacrificial worship at the Temple of God in Jerusalem. Human sacrifices were forbidden, because it would have been murder. The only human sacrifice God accepted was the offering of His only begotten Son, Jesus Christ, who was both God and man, and who knew no sin.

Although the Nabateans appeared to be a benign and civilized society, yet there is some evidence that their priests offered up human life at the high place, as well as other places in their kingdom. Al Uzza, the morning star goddess, is thought to have called for the sacrifice of boys and girls. The philosopher Porphyrius reported that once a year, a boy's throat was cut in a sacrificial ceremony. There is also a Nabatean chronicle at Hegra which states: "Abd-Wadd, priest of Wadd, and his son Salim, and Zayd-Wadd, have consecrated the young man Salim to be immolated [sacrificed] to Dhu Gabat. Their double happiness."

From the preceding Nabatean record, it would appear that it was considered a great honor to be chosen, or to volunteer, for sacrifice. However, it would appear that both the Edomites and Nabateans worshiped the same gods and goddesses as the Babylonians, Egyptians, Greeks, and other civilizations, with only the names of these pagan deities being changed. All can be traced back to a common source, Nimrod and Babylon.

To understand the mystery religion of Babylon, we should first understand that all the gods of the Chaldeans sprang from the legend of Nimrod. In *The Two Babylons,* Alexander Hislop wrote in great detail concerning the evolvement of the religion of Babylon through the founder of Babel. Concerning some of the gods and goddesses, we quote from the book *Babylon* by John Oates:

> The roots of Babylonian religion lie far back in the prehistoric past. Anu . . . who appears as a shadowy figure throughout Mesopotamian history, originally stood at its head. . . . Under various names Ishtar was later to become the most important goddess throughout Western Asia. . . . In late Babylonian times the title Bel, Lord, became synonymous with Marduk, who like Ishtar assimilated to himself various aspects of other gods. A second group of gods consisted of the astral deities, the Sun, the Moon, and the planet Venus. Of these the moon-god Sin was perhaps the most important. . . . Ishtar, goddess of love and war, was, like Shamash, a child of the moon-god. She was Venus, the Morning and Evening Star, and she often was represented riding on her sacred beast, the lion. . . . Closely associated with Ishtar, but whose rank in the pantheon is obscure, is Tammuz . . . whose death and disappearance it was custom to mourn. Much has been written

about Tammuz and the mythology associated with his name on the assumption that he underwent an annual resurrection.

Another principal Babylonian god was Sin, the sun god, whose worship was often accompanied with the lighting of candles. There were many other gods in the Babylonian pantheon, and the religion of Babylon included amulets to ward off evil spirits and sacrifices to demons. Marduk was the same as Baal of the Canaanites, and Ishtar was the Diana of the Ephesians and the Grecian world. All the gods of Babylon can be traced to the idols and gods of Greece, Rome, Egypt, and the heathen world. Hinduism and Buddhism are much like, in part, the mystery religion of Babylon.

After Nimrod died, according to the Babylonian tradition, his wife Semiramis bore a son whom she named Tammuz. She claimed that Tammuz was Nimrod reborn, the son of the sun god. This was a satanic deception of the promise of a coming Savior in Genesis 3:15: "And I will put enmity between thee and the woman, and between thy seed and her seed; it shall bruise thy head, and thou shalt bruise his heel." The resurrection of Tammuz was, of course, another part of the satanic lie. Semiramis claimed that her son was supernaturally conceived, so the mother was worshipped as well as the child. Many of the Jews in Babylon accepted, at least in part, this satanic religion. One of the Jewish months is named Tammuz. We read in Ezekiel 8:14–15:

Then he brought me to the door of the gate of the LORD's house which was toward the north; and, behold, there sat women weeping for Tammuz. Then said he unto me, Hast thou seen this, O son of man? turn thee yet again, and thou shalt see greater abominations than these.

Concerning the spread of the mystery religion of Babylon, we quote from the book *Babylon Mystery Religion* by Ralph Woodrow:

> The Chinese had a mother goddess called Shingmoo or the "Holy Mother." She is pictured with child in arms and rays of glory around her head. The ancient Germans worshipped the virgin Hertha with child in arms. The Scandinavians called her Disa, who was also pictured with child. The Etruscans called her Nutria and among the Druids the Virgo-Patitura was worshipped as the "Mother of God." In India, she was known as Indrani, who also was represented with child in arms. The mother goddess was known as Aphrodite to the Greeks; Nana, to the Sumerians; and as Venus to her devotees in the olden days of Rome, and her child was Jupiter. . . . In Asia, the mother was known as Cybele and the child as Deoius.
>
> "But regardless of her name or place," says one writer, "she was the wife of Baal, the virgin queen of heaven, who bore fruit although she never conceived." When the children of Israel fell into apostasy, they too were defiled with this mother goddess worship. As we read in Judges 2:13, "They forsook the Lord, and served Baal and Ashtaroth."
>
> . . . One of the titles by which the goddess was known among them was "the queen of heaven" (Jer. 44:17–19). …The prophet Jeremiah rebuked them for worshipping her. . . . In Ephesus, the great mother was known as Diana. The temple dedicated to her in that city was one of the seven wonders of the an-

cient world! Not only at Ephesus, but throughout all Asia and the world was the goddess worshipped (Acts 19:27). In Egypt, the mother was known as Isis and her child as Horus. . . . This false worship, having spread from Babylon to the various nations, in different names and forms, finally became established at Rome and throughout the Roman Empire.

It should also be noted that many of the idols of Diana by the idol makers at Ephesus were made with a replica of the Tower of Babel on top of her head, recognizing the false religion of Babylon and that the goddess was actually the wife of Nimrod. The worship of the pseudo-goddess and her offspring in all nations can be traced back to Babel and the incorporation of this satanic deception into the mystery religion of Babylon. Israel and Judah were warned repeatedly by the prophets of God to reject this prostitution by the devil of the promise of a coming Redeemer, but they continued to follow the false prophets of Baal such as Jezebel. Finally, God allowed them first to be subjugated by Assyria, and then by Babylon from whence the religion came.

Isaiah repeatedly warned Israel against worshipping the gods and goddesses of Babylon, but then the prophet pointed to the birth of the true Savior of God: ". . . Hear ye now, O house of David; Is it a small thing for you to weary men, but will ye weary my God also? Therefore the Lord himself shall give you a sign; Behold, a virgin shall conceive, and bear a son, and shall call his name Immanuel" (Isa. 7:13–14).

In the fullness of time, a virgin by the name of Mary did conceive and bear a Son by the Holy Ghost. Certainly Mary was a handmaiden of the Lord, specially chosen according to time, circumstances, and heritage to bring the

Savior into the world to save sinners. She is to be called blessed by all who receive Jesus Christ as Lord and Savior. But there is no scripture in all the Bible that even implies that her birth was of a divine nature, that she was sinless, that she was caught up to Heaven, or that she is to be worshipped or prayed to by Christians. None of the apostles or disciples worshipped her or directed intercessions before God to her. There is not one single word of evidence in the records of the early church that Mary was worshipped or considered more than being the mother of the Lord. "For there is one God, and one mediator between God and men, the man Christ Jesus; Who gave himself a ransom for all, to be testified in due time" (1 Tim. 2:5–6).

The *Encyclopaedia Britannica* states that in the Christian churches of the first centuries, no emphasis was placed upon the worship of Mary. The *Catholic Encyclopedia* reports:

> Devotion to our Blessed Lady in its ultimate analysis must be regarded as a practical application of the doctrine of the Communion of Saints. Seeing that this doctrine is not contained, at least explicitly, in the earlier forms of the Apostles' Creed, there is perhaps no ground for surprise if we do not meet with any clear traces of the cultus of the Blessed Virgin in the first Christian centuries.

It was not until Emperor Constantine made Christianity the state religion of the Roman Empire that Mariology became an important part of church doctrine. Because of the Babylonish religion that had spread to all the world, it became easier for the heathen world to profess allegiance to the state church if the main beliefs in the traditions of Nimrod could be incorporated into worship. In A.D. 431 at the Council of Ephesus, the worship of Mary in the form that is prevalent today was adopted as an official church doctrine.

In the book *Babylon Mystery Religion*, the author states:

> A further indication that Mary worship developed out of the old worship of the mother goddess may be seen in the titles by which the Babylonian goddess was known. In deified form, Nimrod came to be known as Baal. The title of his wife, the female divinity, would be the equivalent of Baalti. In English, the word means "My Lady"; in Latin, "Mea Domina"; and in Italian, it is corrupted into the well-known "Madonna"!

Therefore, it is no mystery that the government of Iraq has stated that the rock star Madonna of the United States lives in the heart of the Iraqi people, and why she was invited to reign as queen over the Festival of Babylon in 1987 (*Los Angeles Times,* January 16, 1987).

Other evidences that shed further light on the religion of Petra's past inhabitants are the obelisks which sprang up throughout the city. Two of the more prominent obelisks are located on the Attuf Ridge and were made by cutting the entire mountain top away, leaving the two objects protruding toward the sky.

In the case of Nimrod, according to the tradition as related by some ancient sources, all of the body was cut up and scattered with the exception of his reproductive organs. It was from this ancient and obscure Babylonian tradition that the worship of the "phallus" began.

In Genesis 10 we read that Ham begat Cush, and Cush begat Nimrod. The next great king of Babylon to arise after Nimrod was Hammurabi, his name signifying that he was a descendant of Nimrod through Ham. The laws of Hammurabi were graven on a large black stone in the shape of a phallus.

In Egypt, Semiramis took the name of Isis, and Tammuz became Horus. The *Encyclopedia of Religions* (Vol. 3, p. 264) states that Queen Semiramis in Babylon erected an obelisk 130 feet high to the memory of Nimrod. Such temples were common in Babylon and later Egypt. These obelisks are replete in the temples of Luxor and Karnak. Many of the monuments have been removed to other nations. One stands in Central Park in New York City, one in London, and others in Italy.

According to *The Two Babylons* by Hislop, and *Babylon Mystery Religion* by Woodrow, these obelisks, or standing images as they were called in the Hebrew, are mentioned in both 1 Kings and 2 Kings as a part of Baal worship. Baal is one of the names for Nimrod. It was into this kind of evil and licentious religion that Jezebel enticed Israel. It is to the abolition of the last vestiges of the Babylonian idolatry that Isaiah 27:1,9 is addressed:

> In that day the LORD with his sore and great and strong sword shall punish leviathan the piercing serpent, even leviathan that crooked serpent; and he shall slay the dragon that is in the sea. . . . By this therefore shall the iniquity of Jacob be purged; and this is all the fruit to take away his sin; when he maketh all the stones of the altar as chalkstones that are beaten in sunder, the groves and images shall not stand up.

A common practice in Egypt, Greece, and other nations of the Middle East and the Mediterranean area where the religion of Babylon had spread, was to erect an obelisk in front of the temple. This symbolism for the phallus associated the religion with the fertility cult of Nimrod. The temples of Diana, the Ephesian counterpart of Nimrod's wife, the queen of heaven, was supported by the temple prostitutes. According to Ezekiel 8:1–6, this abominable symbol was erected in front of the Temple at the north gate. Ezekiel referred to it as the "image of jealousy." We can be certain that it was the Babylonian symbol of Nimrod because we read in verse fourteen that the prophet saw a woman at the Temple weeping for Tammuz, the son of Nimrod.

Emperor Caligula was one of the most cruel and degenerate of the caesars of Rome. According to the book *Babylon Mystery Religion,* Caligula transported an obelisk from Heliopolis in Egypt to the section of Rome which was called his *circus.* This hill is the place where the Vatican was later built. The obelisk remained in the Vatican until 1586 when Pope Sixtus V had it moved in front of St. Peter's Cathedral where it is today. The pope had decreed the death penalty if it should be broken or damaged. The mover was a man named Domenico Fontana. Forty-five winches, 160 horses, and a crew of 800 men were required to move the obelisk to its new location. When the task was completed, the pope blessed it and the workmen who had moved it under such an extreme penalty for failure. An inscription in the pagan temple of Heliopolis, from where the obelisk came, reads: "I, Dionysus, dedicated these phalli to Hera, my stepmother." The account of the moving of the obelisk can be found in Hasting's *Encyclopedia of Religion and Ethics* in a section on phallicism.

It is also interesting to take note that the obelisk in front of St. Peter's Cathedral came from Heliopolis. We read in Jeremiah 43:13, "He shall break also the images of

A half-view of the Treasury Building that greets tourists coming through the El Ciq. Note the height in contrast to the people on the steps.

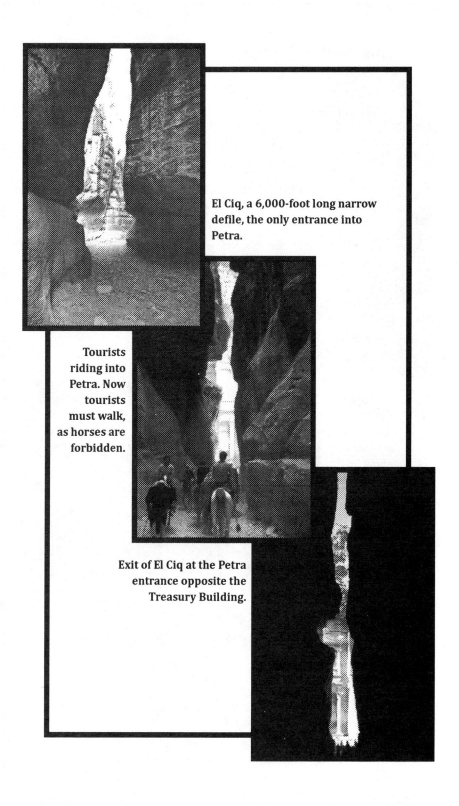

El Ciq, a 6,000-foot long narrow defile, the only entrance into Petra.

Tourists riding into Petra. Now tourists must walk, as horses are forbidden.

Exit of El Ciq at the Petra entrance opposite the Treasury Building.

A view of the Roman Theatre from a cave, possibly built by Marc Antony for Cleopatra.

A theatre marking Roman control of Petra from about 50 B.C. to A.D. 500.

Close-up of detail of the Treasury Building.

The Dead Sea

Southern end of the Dead Sea

One of the thousands of cave dwellings in Petra.

Camels are still a beast of burden for bedouins in Petra.

Some of the architecture in Petra is of various origins: Horite, Edomite, Nabatean, Persian, and Roman.

Two views of Aaron's tomb on top of Mount Hor. This is a most holy place to Muslims.

Observing Jews daily go to the remains of the Temple's Western Wall to pray for the coming of Messiah.

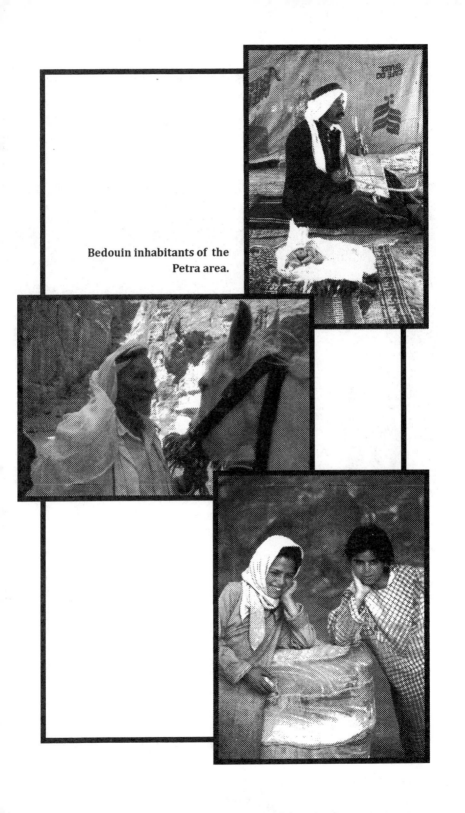

Bedouin inhabitants of the
Petra area.

My November 2008 tour group in Petra.

Beth-shemesh, that is in the land of Egypt; and the houses of the gods of the Egyptians shall he burn with fire." The footnote in the *Pilgrim Bible* on Beth-shemesh reads, "This means 'House of the Sun,' or temples dedicated to sun-worship. . . . This was probably the city which was called Heliopolis by the Greeks."

Wherever we have gone in the world, we have seen the obelisk in its relationship to the mystery religion of Babylon. In China we saw the entire land punctuated with Buddhist shrines called *pagodas.* These pagodas rise high in the sky in tiers, much like the Tower of Babel, and the phallus symbol of Nimrod. In China, Semiramis, the mother goddess, was called Shingmoo. Throughout the Muslim world from Morocco, to Egypt, to Syria, Jordan, and Iraq, we have seen mosques surrounded by minarets, slender spires with an enlarged section at the top. The symbolism is apparent. Mecca, in the heart of Islam, fractures the skyline with a host of minarets with their slight enlargements at the apex.

In the fourth and fifth centuries, the Roman Empire divided into two parts, with Constantinople becoming the capital city of the eastern leg. The church at St. Sophia was the pride of the Holy Byzantine Empire. In front of St. Sophia in the town square is an obelisk, the twin of the one at St. Peter's. This obelisk is still standing today. When we were in Istanbul, our guide informed us that it was at this obelisk where doctrinal disagreements were settled through athletic contests. After the Turks captured Constantinople on May 29, 1453, and changed the name to Istanbul, St. Sophia was converted to a mosque and minarets were erected around it.

In temples, shrines, mosques, and churches of all religions of the world, obelisk-like spires and towers are included in construction. Many of these elongated units simply follow tradition without any realization of their meaning or relationship to the mystery religion of Babylon.

The obelisk in front of St. Peter's in Rome, including the foundation, is 132 feet high. Inasmuch as it came from Heliopolis in Egypt, it is probably no coincidence that it is approximately the same height as the one that Queen Semiramis erected in honor of her husband, Nimrod. But the largest obelisk in the world is in front of our nation's capitol building in Washington, D.C.—the Washington Monument. Again, it was probably no coincidence that the phallus-shaped obelisk was chosen to memorialize George Washington as the father of the United States.

As we consider the major religions of mankind, there are literally hundreds of connections that could be made to the mystery religion of Babylon. The most prominent, besides the obelisk, is the worship of idols, or the use of idols in worship.

As evil as the thoughts and deeds of mankind became in the millennium before the flood, there is no evidence that idol worship was among its sins. Idol worship originated at Babel, and after Babel, as the people were scattered over the face of the earth, they carried with them this religious abomination. Throughout Egypt, the Hebrews were confronted with idols to the Egyptian gods, which in reality were only Babylonian gods that had been given Egyptian names. When they passed through the land of the Canaanite tribes, they saw similar idols which had been given Canaanite names. Therefore, the Lord gave this commandment to Moses for the Israelites: "Ye shall make you no idols nor graven image, neither rear you up a standing image, neither shall ye set up any image of stone in your land, to bow down unto it: for I am the Lord your God" (Lev. 26:1).

The Babylonian concept of idol worship was the chief weapon of Satan that the prophets of God had to contend with. There are thousands of references in the Old Testament alone to idol worship. Like a large segment of both Catholic and non-Catholic Christendom today, the Hebrews tried to make a pretense of worshipping God while catering to their idolatry. We read in Jeremiah 7:8–10,18,30–31:

> Behold, ye trust in lying words, that cannot profit. Will ye steal, murder, and commit adultery, and swear falsely, and burn incense unto Baal, and walk after other gods whom ye know not; And come and stand before me in this house, which is called by my name, and say, We are delivered to do all these abominations? ... The children gather wood, and the fathers kindle the fire, and the women knead their dough, to make cakes to the queen of heaven, and to pour out drink offerings unto other gods, that they may provoke me to anger. ... For the children of Judah have done evil in my sight, saith the LORD: they have set their abominations in the house which is called by my name, to pollute it. And they have built the high places of Tophet, which is in the valley of the son of Hinnom, to burn their sons and their daughters in the fire; which I commanded them not. ...

It was the worship of idols, mainly Baal (Nimrod) and the queen of heaven (Nimrod's wife) that brought the judgment of God upon the nation. In the early church it was idol worshippers and makers at Ephesus and other cities who were the fiercest enemies of the disciples. In Athens, the city was overrun with idols, so much so that they even had an idol to the unknown god! In Rome, at the

Parthenon, there were idols to every god in the known world.

Like the Israelites, there were some in the early church who professed Jesus Christ as Lord and Savior, yet clung to their heathen idols. We read of this abomination in 2 Corinthians 6:15–17:

> And what concord hath Christ with Belial? or what part hath he that believeth with an infidel? And what agreement hath the temple of God with idols? . . . Wherefore come out from among them, and be ye separate, saith the Lord, and touch not the unclean thing; and I will receive you.

In India, the Hindu temples are filled with idols of the Babylonian fertility cult; in Bangkok, the temples are likewise filled with idols; in China, the Buddhist temples have the largest idols in the world. After the Council of Ephesus in A.D. 431 sanctioned the worship of the godmother religion, the churches of Asia became filled with idols. When Mohammed ravaged the churches of this territory early in the seventh century, he brought fifteen hundred idols back to Mecca. Regardless how identifiable statues are with Christianity, it is an abomination to worship and kiss them. We read in 1 Kings 19:18, ". . . I have left me seven thousand in Israel, all the knees which have not bowed unto Baal, and every mouth which hath not kissed him." Kissing an idol is associated with the worship of Baal, or Nimrod.

Considering Petra's idolatrous past in comparison to the glory of Israel when Jesus Christ returns to build His Temple and reign on David's throne, we understand even more fully the reason for God's attitude: ". . . Jacob have I loved . . . Esau have I hated. . . ."

FROM MEDO-PERSIA TO ROME

I n continuing our study on Petra in history and prophecy, we consider next the status of Petra under the Persian Empire. After the defeat of Babylon, Medo-Persia extended its empire from India to Egypt. However, there is little evidence that more than peripheral attention was given to Petra. The Medes and Persians were initially occupied with consolidating and governing the many nations and peoples that had been suddenly put under their domination, and later with extending the empire to Greece. While some of the facades on the stone buildings in Petra do imitate Persian architecture, this was probably due to imported Persian influence rather than by occupying forces.

Cyrus of Persia did allow several contingents of Jews to return and rebuild the Temple, and in 455 B.C. Artaxerxes signed a decree to permit the rebuilding of Jerusalem. The problems presented by the Edomites at this time came from those living to the east and south of Jerusalem. The Nabateans appeared to mind their own business.

Petra During the Grecian Empire
In 333 B.C., Alexander of Greece crossed over into Asia

and marched southward along the Mediterranean coast. His primary goal was to destroy the bases from which the large Persian navy operated. He met the bulk of the monstrous Persian army at Issus and destroyed it. He later passed through Israel on the way to Egypt in haste to get rid of his last obstacle, the large Persian base at what is now Alexandria. On his way back through Israel, he had more important things on his mind than an isolated rockbound city two hundred miles to the south. From Jerusalem, he turned north and east to invade Persia.

After Alexander's death in 323 B.C., his empire was divided into four parts, with each being given to one of his four generals. Petra then belonged to Syria. Seleucus sent several expeditions to take Petra, but the city was too strongly defended for the Greeks to take. In 312 B.C. Antigonus of Syria made another attempt. He waited until Petra's regional trade fair was in progress, moved swiftly into Petra, seized a large quantity of gold, precious stones, and livestock, and then fled. The Nabateans quickly reacted. According to the historian Siculus, the Nabateans caught the exhausted Greeks sleeping, and of the force of eight thousand, only fifty escaped.

The Nabateans made a peace proposition to Antigonus, which he accepted. He again tried to take Petra by surprise with a force of four thousand cavalry, but the Greeks failed again. After this debacle, the Nabateans were granted an autonomous status.

In the fifth and ninth chapters of 1 Maccabees, the Nabateans are described as being the Jews' friends; however, friction later developed when they extended their kingdom as far north as Bashan, known today as the Golan Heights. As the Ptolemies of Egypt and the Seleucids of Syria began to lose power, the Nabateans annexed portions of Syria and even launched a campaign against

Egypt. However, the Romans were moving into the Middle East and any further empire designs of Petra were short lived.

Petra During the Roman Empire

In 85 B.C., the Nabateans came into contact with the Romans, and as in the past, they did not submit meekly. It was not until thirty years later that Sabinus, the administrator of Syria, was finally able to defeat them. Subsequently, Marc Antony was made the Roman ruler of the entire Middle East, and in 32 B.C. he gave Petra to Cleopatra of Egypt as a gift.

After Marc Antony had solidified his hold on all Asia and defeated his republican enemies at Philippi, he went to Egypt where he met Cleopatra in 42 B.C. Forgetting about his wife, Fulvia, in Rome, he entered into an extended adulterous relationship with Cleopatra, who was actually Grecian and not Egyptian. The relationship between the two was a matter of extreme displeasure with Octavian and the Senate. Fulvia died, or was killed, in 40 B.C. To heal the breach with Rome, Antony married Octavian's sister, Octavia. In 37 B.C., Antony returned to Egypt and made Alexandria his headquarters. The relationship with Cleopatra was resumed to the extent that she seemed to dominate the Roman's will.

How much time Cleopatra and Marc Antony spent in Petra is not known. Doubtless the two visited the city, as he presented it to her as a gift. Cleopatra must have loved the city very much, and it is possible that Antony built the Roman theatre that still stands in Petra to please her.

Giving this important city of Rome to the Egyptian queen must have further infuriated Octavian, as in the same year, 32 B.C., the Senate stripped Antony of all authority and ordered him to return to Rome. Civil war ensued and the forces of Antony were defeated. He committed suicide in 30 B.C., and shortly afterward, Cleopatra took her own life.

Thus we see the part that Petra may have played in this historical human drama, as well as providing background inspiration for William Shakespeare's play *Antony and Cleopatra.*

About the time that Antony and Cleopatra committed suicide, Herod the Great, an Edomite, was made king of Judah by Caesar. Herod got into trouble at home and fled for his life to Petra. He was refused entry by the Nabateans, and consequently went to Rome and the Senate reinstated him to power. The Jews considered it a supreme insult for an Edomite to be made king over them. He was the king of Israel when Jesus was born. After his death, his son Herod Philip took his throne, and to his dominion was added Edom and Petra. However, the Nabateans did not like him either, and both Herods were at war continually with the rebelling Nabateans.

Nevertheless, the Romans were very thorough in their use of conquered territories and peoples. They made Petra into one of the most important trade centers in the world. Through Petra poured goods and merchandise of all kinds from Persia, India, Ethiopia, and some believe as far away as China. Pliny wrote that all kinds of spices, silks, dyes, gold, pearls, and precious stones were brought to Petra to be shipped to Rome and sold in the markets. The historian also noted that from Petra, three million dollars a year was added to the Roman treasury, and in those days this sum would amount to a large amount of money.

While under the protection and influence of Rome, the Nabateans evidently became affluent, and not having to provide arms for their own protection or economy, they became dependent. When Rome began to break up and the Roman legions left in the fifth century, Petra as a trade center declined, and the Nabateans, having lost their pride and self-reliance, once again melted away into the wilderness from where they had come. When the Moslems marched through Israel, and what is now Jordan in the seventh century, no mention is made of Petra or the Nabateans in any record of their conquests and exploits. Therefore, it must have become a ghost town by the year A.D. 625, a home for wandering Bedouin tribes until it was visited by Burckhardt in 1812.

The Romans left their mark in the architecture of Petra. Rows of Roman columns that supported buildings are still standing in what was once the center of the Petra complex, and a Roman theater is for the most part intact, located about five hundred yards from the Treasury Building at the entrance to the Ciq.

The last king of Petra was Rabel, who died in A.D. 106, and it was after this that the Nabateans lost their identity as a race. In the second and third centuries, Christianity was brought to Petra by the early disciples. Some of the temples were converted into churches, and early church annals listed several bishops of Petra, of whom the more prominent were Eusebius and Jerome. But any Christian influence there in Petra was swept away by the Muslim tide that inundated the Middle East by Mohammed and his followers.

Even though Petra as an identifiable place of any importance became isolated from the outside world, separated unto itself by mountains, deserts, and areas of emptiness, the cave dwellings and valuable water source still provided a base for the remnant of the Nabatean tribes. As referenced previously, the present local inhabitants fiercely defend their Nabatean heritage.

GOD'S JUDGMENT UPON PETRA

The judgment that God ordained against the citadel of Esau in Isaiah 34 contains a double meaning—the desolate state of Petra as it would remain during the times of Jewish dispersion into all nations until they returned and it became a possession of Israel. Isaiah 34:5,8–17 says:

For my sword shall be bathed in heaven: behold, it shall come down upon Idumea, and upon the people of my curse, to judgment. . . . For it is the day of the LORD's vengeance, and the year of recompences for the controversy of Zion. And the streams thereof shall be turned into pitch, and the dust thereof into brimstone, and the land thereof shall become burning pitch. It shall not be quenched night nor day; the smoke thereof shall go up for ever: from generation to generation it shall lie waste; none shall pass through it for ever and ever. But the cormorant and the bittern shall possess it; the owl also and the raven shall dwell in it: and he shall stretch out upon it the line of confusion, and the stones of emptiness. They shall call the nobles thereof to the kingdom, but none shall be there, and all her princes shall be nothing. And thorns shall come up in her palaces, nettles and brambles in the fortresses thereof: and it shall be an habitation of dragons, and a court for owls. The wild beasts of the desert shall also meet with the wild beasts of the island, and the satyr shall cry to his fellow; the screech owl also shall rest there, and find for herself a place of rest. There shall the great owl make her nest, and lay, and hatch, and gather under her shadow: there shall the vultures also be gathered, every one with her mate. Seek ye out of the book of the LORD, and read: no one of these shall fail.... And he hath cast the lot for them, and his hand hath divided it unto them by line: they shall possess it for ever, from generation to generation shall they dwell therein.

God's edict concerning Petra was that it would lay empty, barren, and waste, but in the day of the Lord, Israel would possess it for an everlasting habitation.

Another prophecy concerning the past and future of Petra is given in Malachi 1:2–5:

I have loved you, saith the LORD. Yet ye say, Wherein hast thou loved us? Was not Esau Jacob's brother? saith the LORD: yet I loved Jacob, And I hated Esau, and laid his mountains and his heritage waste for the dragons of the wilderness. Whereas Edom saith, We are impoverished, but we will return and build the desolate places; thus saith the LORD of hosts, They shall build, but I will throw down; and they shall call them, The border of wickedness, and, The people against whom the LORD hath indignation for ever. And your eyes shall see, and ye shall say, The LORD will be magnified from the border of Israel.

In modern Jordan today, the ancient cities like Philadelphia (Amman) and Ezion-geber (Aqaba) have been rebuilt and enlarged, but Petra remains a desolation. It has been built and rebuilt many times, but God has always intervened and made it desolate again. According to prophecy, it will remain as it is today until the descendants of Jacob claim it.

We read also of Edom and Petra in Ezekiel 25:12–14:

Thus saith the Lord GOD; Because that Edom hath dealt against the house of Judah by taking vengeance, and hath greatly offended, and revenged himself upon them; Therefore thus saith the Lord GOD; I will also stretch out mine hand upon Edom, and will cut off man and beast from it; and I will make it desolate from Teman; and they of Dedan shall fall by the sword. And I will lay my vengeance upon Edom by the hand of my people Israel: and they shall do in Edom according to mine anger and according to my fury; and they shall know my vengeance, saith the Lord GOD.

God gave the Edomites a thousand years to come to the knowledge of the truth that He is God and accept the covenant He made with Jacob to live in peace with Israel. However, they would not. The Edomites killed the Jews and claimed the land that God gave them during the time of their supreme calamity, the Babylonian captivity. He moved Ezekiel to pronounce the final judgment upon them. The following warning against Mount Seir applies to all nations who persecute Israel. If Israel needs to be punished for their transgressions, then God will do it, but woe unto that nation which attempts to take the judgment of the Jews upon itself:

Moreover the word of the LORD came unto me, saying, Son of man, set thy face against mount Seir, and prophesy against it, And say unto it, Thus saith the Lord GOD; Behold, O mount Seir, I am against thee, and I will stretch out mine hand against thee, and I will make thee most desolate. I will lay thy cities waste, and thou shalt be desolate, and thou shalt know that I am the LORD. Because thou hast had a perpetual hatred, and hast shed the blood of the children of Israel by the force of the sword in the time of their calamity, in the time that their iniquity had an end: ...I will make thee perpetual desolations, and thy cities shall not return: and ye shall know that I am the LORD. . . . And thou shalt know that I am the LORD, and that I have heard all thy blasphemies which thou hast spoken against the mountains of Israel, saying, They are laid desolate, they are given us to consume. Thus with your mouth ye have boasted against me, and have multiplied your words against me: I have heard them. Thus saith the Lord GOD; When the whole earth rejoiceth, I will make thee desolate. As thou didst rejoice at the inheritance of the house of Israel, because it was desolate, so will I do unto thee: thou shalt be desolate, O mount Seir, and all Idumea, even all of it: and they shall know that I am the LORD.

—Ezekiel 35:1–5,9,12–15

There are more judgments of God declared against the descendants of Esau and Mount Seir in the Bible than any other nation or race. There are entire chapters in Jeremiah, Isaiah, Ezekiel, and the minor prophets that prophesy against Edom, Mount Seir, and the Edomites that we have not even referred to in this study. The book of Obadiah is a declaration of God's wrath against Edom and Esau. We read in Obadiah 10,17–21:

> For thy violence against thy brother Jacob shame
> shall cover thee, and thou shalt be cut off for ever. . . .
> But upon mount Zion shall be deliverance, and there
> shall be holiness; and the house of Jacob shall possess
> their possessions. And the house of Jacob shall be a
> fire, and the house of Joseph a flame, and the house
> of Esau for stubble, and they shall kindle in them, and
> devour them; and there shall not be any remaining of
> the house of Esau; for the LORD hath spoken it. And
> they of the south shall possess the mount of Esau; and
> they of the plain the Philistines: and they shall pos-
> sess the fields of Ephraim, and the fields of Samaria:
> and Benjamin shall possess Gilead. And the captivity
> of this host of the children of Israel shall possess that
> of the Canaanites, even unto Zarephath; and the cap-
> tivity of Jerusalem, which is in Sepharad, shall possess
> the cities of the south. And saviours shall come up on
> mount Zion to judge the mount of Esau; and the king-
> dom shall be the LORD's.

While the prophecies against Mount Seir foretell an extended period of desolation, at the same time they indicate that the enmity between the descendants of Esau
and the descendants of Jacob could continue until God
establishes His Kingdom on earth, with Jesus Christ as
King, and judges appointed to judge the nations in their
relationship to Israel. In that day, according to Obadiah,
the Edomites will be judged and utterly cast out.

When the Romans destroyed Jerusalem, killing a million Jews and dispersing the rest into other nations, there
is no indication in Josephus, or any other records that we
can find, of the disposition of the Edomites who lived in

the land. We know that the Romans favored the Edomites because they placed four Edomite kings upon the throne of Judah. As we have already noted, there is strong evidence that the Palestinians today who cause Israel so much trouble are of Edomite ancestry. We read in Amos 9:11–12:

> In that day will I raise up the tabernacle of David that is fallen, and close up the breaches thereof; and I will raise up his ruins, and I will build it as in the days of old: That they may possess the remnant of Edom, and of all the heathen, which are called by my name, saith the LORD that doeth this.

THE LAND GOD GAVE ISRAEL

About the time that Petra disappeared into history for a thousand years, a new religion was born within the Arab world. We quote from page 88 of the book Jordan— A Country Study by the American University, Washington, D.C.:

> In A.D. 610 Muhammed, a merchant belonging to the Hashemite branch of the ruling Quraysh tribe in the Arabian town of Mecca, began to preach the first of a series of revelations, granted by God through the angel Gabriel. . . . In 622 he was invited to . . . Medina. . . . The Muslim calendar, based on the lunar year, begins in 622. In Media, Muhammed—by this time known as the Prophet—continued to preach, eventually defeated his detractors in battle, and consolidated both the temporal and spiritual leadership of all Arabia in his person before his death in 632.

Supposedly, the king of Jordan, King Hussein, was a descendant of the Hashemite family from which Muhammed came, and he also claimed to be a direct descendant of the Arabian prophet. In fact, most ruling monarchs of the Arab nations claim to have descended from Muhammed. On page 19 of *Jordan—A Country Study,* the genealogy of the Hashemite family from which many of the Arab rulers belong is traced to Hussein ibn Ali, born in 1852 and died in 1931. This is why Jordan is known as the Hashemite kingdom. The ruling family claims to be descendants of Muhammed, the Hashemite.

In the latter half of the nineteenth century, Palestine was under British administration, and the Jews were permitted to buy land from the Palestinians. The movement of Jews back to the land was promoted by the World Zionist Organization. Gradually, large tracts of land came under Jewish ownership in the Jerusalem and Tel Aviv areas, and this was prophesied in the Bible. While Jeremiah 32 initially refers to the return of the Jews after the Babylonian captivity, its greater and final application is to Israel in these last days:

> Behold, I will gather them out of all countries, whither I have driven them in mine anger, and in my fury, and in great wrath; and I will bring them again unto this place, and I will cause them to dwell safely: . . . **Men shall buy fields for money,** and subscribe evidences, and seal them, and take witnesses in the land of Benjamin, and in the places about Jerusalem, and in the cities of Judah, and in the cities of the mountains, and in the cities of the valley, and in the cities of the south: for I will cause their captivity to return, saith the LORD.
>
> —Jeremiah 32:37,44

The Balfour Declaration

During the First World War, Lord Balfour, the distinguished English statesman, served as foreign secretary of Great Britain. From about 1300 to 1919, the Turkish Empire, also known as the Ottoman Empire, dominated North Africa, Southeast Asia, and the Middle East. In the

First World War, Turkey fought with Germany. With the defeat of Germany, Turkey subsequently lost and all its conquered territories for the most part were put at the disposal of England. Besides being a politician, Lord Balfour was also somewhat of a theologian, having written and published a book entitled *Theism and Thought: A Study in Familiar Beliefs.* Lord Balfour doubtless prevailed on the British government to remember the aspiration of the Zionist organization in dividing up Turkish territories. We quote from the book *Hashemite Kingdom of Jordan:*

> The outbreak of war had effectively prevented any further development of Zionist settlements in Palestine, and the main efforts of this cause shifted to England, where discussion with Zionists was seen as having potential value to the pursuit of British war aims. The protracted negotiations with the British foreign office was climaxed on November 2, 1917, by the letter from Foreign Secretary Arthur James Balfour that became known as the Balfour Declaration. This document declared the British government's "sympathy with Jewish Zionist aspirations," viewed with favor "the establishment in Palestine of a national home for the Jewish people," and announced an intent to "facilitate the achievement of this object, it being clearly understood that nothing shall be done which may prejudice the civil and religious rights of existing non-Jewish communities in Palestine."

In September 1918 the British army decisively defeated the Turkish army at Megiddo. After that, there were a number of conferences and commissions to decide the puzzle-like composition of the Middle East. There was much political pressure among the Arab leaders to block the formation of a Jewish state; however, the Supreme Allied Council at San Remo in April 1920, under the terms of the Palestine Mandate, out of the Ottoman Empire created Syria and Lebanon under the authority of the French, and Iraq under the British. The Palestine Mandate also reaffirmed the Balfour Declaration, and called on the mandatory power to "secure establishment of the Jewish national home."

Under the loosely defined boundaries for the provisions of a Jewish homeland in the Balfour Declaration, the territories of Israel under the reign of David and Solomon were recognized. This would have included Lebanon, part of Syria, almost all of what is now Jordan, and the Sinai region. However, T. E. Lawrence, also known as Lawrence of Arabia, had made many promises to the Arabs in World War I in order to enlist their aid in fighting the Turks. We quote from *Jordan—A Country Study:*

In March 1921, Winston Churchill, then British colonial secretary, convened a high-level conference in Cairo to consider Middle East policy. As a result of these declarations, Britain subdivided the Palestine Mandate along the Jordan River-Gulf of Aqaba line. The eastern portion—called Transjordan—was to have separate Arab administration operating under the general supervision of the commissioner of Palestine. ... A British government memorandum in September 1922, approved by the League of Nations Council, specifically excluded Jewish settlements from the Transjordan area of the Palestine Mandate. The whole process was aimed at satisfying wartime pledges made to the Arabs.

Where Moses and Joshua Trod

The covenant that God made with Abraham concerning the deed to the land between the rivers of the Euphrates and the Nile, was further confirmed through Moses and Joshua. There was to be no doubt in anyone's mind, neither Jew nor Gentile, that this land was a divine legacy and no other nation besides Israel was to possess it.

God said to Moses, as recorded in Deuteronomy 11:22–24:

> For if ye shall diligently keep all these commandments which I command you, to do them, to love the LORD your God, to walk in all his ways, and to cleave unto him; Then will the LORD drive out all these nations from before you, and ye shall possess greater nations and mightier than yourselves. Every place whereon the soles of your feet shall tread shall be yours: from the wilderness and Lebanon, from the river, the river Euphrates, even unto the uttermost sea shall your coast be.

In tracing the steps of Moses, we find that he led the children of Israel out of the land of Goshen, which is the Nile delta area adjacent to the Mediterranean Sea. He traveled southward the entire length of the Sinai Peninsula to Mount Sinai and the straits of Sharm el-Sheik. Then Moses led the Israelites northward to Kadesh, where they turned eastward toward Edom.

From Petra, Moses led the camp southward to the sea at Aqaba. According to *Halley's Bible Handbook* and other sources, the Israelites circled Edom and Moab on the east side and approached the Jordan River through Ammon. Moses was not allowed by God to enter Canaan; therefore, the covenant was extended through Joshua. We read in Joshua 1:1–4:

> Now after the death of Moses the servant of the LORD it came to pass, that the LORD spake unto Joshua the son of Nun, Moses' minister, saying, Moses my servant is dead; now therefore arise, go over this Jordan, thou, and all this people, unto the land which I do give to them, even to the children of Israel. Every place that the sole of your foot shall tread upon, that have I given unto you, as I said unto Moses. From the wilderness and this Lebanon even unto the great river, the river Euphrates, all the land of the Hittites, and unto the great sea toward the going down of the sun, shall be your coast.

All the wilderness, the entire Sinai Peninsula, that Moses walked through belongs to Israel. The western two-thirds of Jordan, the Golan Heights, Palestine, Lebanon, and the western two-thirds of Syria belongs to Israel. This is not a question of what I or anyone else believes. It is rather of matter of what God has said.

Israel During the Millennium

The borders of Israel during the Millennium, the thousand-year reign of Jesus Christ upon David's throne, are clearly defined in Ezekiel 47:15–21:

> And this shall be the border of the land toward the north side, from the great sea, the way of Hethlon, as men go to Zedad; Hamath, Berothah, Sibraim, which is between the border of Damascus and the border of Hamath; Hazar-hatticon, which is by the coast of Hauran. And the border from the sea shall be Hazarenan,

the border of Damascus, and the north northward, and the border of Hamath. And this is the north side. And the east side ye shall measure from Hauran, and from Damascus, and from Gilead, and from the land of Israel by Jordan, from the border unto the east sea. And this is the east side. And the south side southward, from Tamar even to the waters of strife in Kadesh, the river to the great sea. And this is the south side southward. The west side also shall be the great sea from the border, till a man come over against Hamath. This is the west side. So shall ye divide this land unto you according to the tribes of Israel.

There is a difference of opinion as to the borders of the land Israel shall possess during the Millennium, because it does not seem to include all the land from the Euphrates to the Nile. However, some of these places mentioned, like Berothah and Sibraim, are difficult to locate today. Also, Hamath was not only a city, it was a province stretching all the way from northern Lebanon to the Euphrates in northern Syria, and a further amplification of the tribal division of land in Ezekiel 48 mentions the coast and borders of Hamath, Hazarenan, etc. Therefore, we see no real difference between the title land deed given by God to Abraham, and later confirmed by Moses and Joshua.

The southern boundary of the land given in Ezekiel 47:19 mentioned "the waters of strife in Kadesh." When Israel was camped at Kadesh-barnea, there was much contention within the camp because of the bad water. Kadesh was the southern boundary of the kingdom during David's reign; however, the feet of Moses trod on the shores at Sharm el-Sheik, the narrow entrance to the Red Sea. These narrow straits have always been waters of strife for Israel because enemies have pirated or blockaded Israeli shipping in this area. It was here that the 1967 war between Israel, Egypt, Syria, and Jordan began. The Egyptian navy blockaded the straits and shelled Israeli ships. From Sharm el-Sheik, the border of Israel will extend up the Egyptian arm of the Red Sea to the Nile just north of Cairo, and include the old land of Goshen where Israel labored during their captivity for four hundred years. Israel possessed all the Sinai after the last war, but the United States forced Israel to return it.

God's Word Is Sure

God has promised that He would cause the Israelites to return to their land in the last days, and all the land that was in the kingdom at its greatest expanse would be theirs. We refer first to God's promise in Jeremiah 30:2-3:

> Thus speaketh the LORD God of Israel, saying, Write thee all the words that I have spoken unto thee in a book. For, lo, the days come, saith the LORD, that I will bring again the captivity of my people Israel and Judah, saith the LORD: and I will cause them to return to the land that I gave to their fathers, and they shall possess it.

We read also in Deuteronomy 30:3,5:

> . . . The LORD thy God will turn thy captivity, and have compassion upon thee, and will return and gather thee from all the nations, whither the LORD thy God hath scattered thee. . . . And the LORD thy God will bring thee into the land which thy fathers possessed, and thou shalt possess it; and he will do thee good, and multiply thee above thy fathers.

Israel is not only to get all the land that was in the kingdom of David, but God promises them even more—the rest of Sinai, the land of Goshen, and all of Lebanon. What about the Jordanians, the Syrians, or the Egyptians living on these lands today? We read in Ezekiel 47:22:

> And it shall come to pass, that ye shall divide it by lot for an inheritance unto you, and to the strangers that sojourn among you, which shall beget children among you: and they shall be unto you as born in the country among the children of Israel; they shall have inheritance with you among the tribes of Israel.

The government of Syria recently released an interesting news announcement to the world news services. In the release, Syria accused Israel of attempting to build a kingdom that would stretch from the Euphrates River to the Nile River. Syria was, of course, attempting to turn world opinion against Israel for these aggressive aims. However, in resisting Israel's right to such lands as the Golan Heights, Lebanon, the Sinai, and even the East Bank of the Jordan, as well as the West Bank, the nations are not resisting Israel; they are resisting God. The second psalm reflects God's attitude toward those nations today who are attempting to stop the sure course of prophecy that will lead to the enthronement of Jesus Christ upon David's throne when He comes again.

The struggle going on today that will eventually involve all nations at the battle of Armageddon is still the controversy of Esau attempting to reclaim his birthright, and Jacob trying to claim what God has given him. ". . . There shall come a Star out of Jacob, and a Sceptre shall rise out of Israel. . . . And Edom shall be a possession, Seir also shall be a possession for his enemies; and Israel shall do valiantly" (Num. 24:17-18).

PETRA IN PROPHETIC PERSPECTIVE

From Babylonian captivity the prophet Ezekiel wrote in Ezekiel 35:14–15:

> Thus saith the Lord GOD; When the whole earth rejoiceth, I will make thee desolate. As thou didst rejoice at the inheritance of the house of Israel, because it was desolate, so will I do unto thee: thou shalt be desolate, O mount Seir, and all Idumea, even all of it: and they shall know that I am the LORD.

God has never forgiven Babylon for the destruction of Jerusalem and the Temple, and His justice will not be satisfied until it is destroyed as Sodom and Gomorrah (Jer. 51:34–36). Likewise, God's wrath against Edom for trying to prevent His plan and purpose for the descendants of Jacob being accomplished is eternal—not because God is unable to forgive, but rather because the Edomites are incapable of accepting His forgiveness: Jacob have I loved; Esau have I hated. When the whole earth rejoices during the Millennium, Petra will continue to be a place of desolation.

There is no indication that Jesus Christ ever visited Petra. In fact, there is no record of Jesus even going to the Dead Sea. He did enter Jericho, a distance of less than five miles north of the Dead Sea. Some have theorized that Jesus was a member of the Essene cult that lived a kibbutz-like existence at Qumran, located at the north end of the Dead Sea. It is possible that John the Baptist was an Essene, but it is highly unlikely that Jesus was a member of this particular cult. In fact, Jesus choosing a taxpayer to be an apostle, mixing with sinners like Zachaeus, and witnessing to the fallen woman at the well, was in direct contrast with the worldly separation philosophy of the Essenes. The boundaries of the ministry of Jesus were Jerusalem, Jericho, Gadara on the east side of the Sea of Galilee, Caesarea Philippi, Tyre, and Sidon. These locations marked the main boundaries of the Jewish nation at the time, and Jesus said in Matthew 15:24, "...I am not sent but unto the lost sheep of the house of Israel." Paul also recognized the initial purpose of the ministry of Jesus in Romans 15:8: "Now I say that Jesus Christ was a minister of the circumcision for the truth of God, to confirm the promises made unto the fathers."

The extension of the supreme mission of Jesus Christ, the Son of God, is stated in John 1:11–12: "He came unto his own [Israel], and his own received him not. But as many as received him [including non-Israelites], to them gave he power to become the sons of God, even to them that believe on his name."

According to the apostle Paul's own words, he received by revelation a message of salvation, a gift from God, to be preached to the Gentiles. This message, or gospel, was void of commandments relating to the keeping of the letter of the law, observing feast days, the Sabbath, sacrifices, and Temple worship. About these forms of worship which looked forward to the Messiah, the Gentiles knew nothing (Eph. 3; Gal. 1–2; etc.). Salvation to the Gentiles was by simple faith, according to God's grace, that God's Son, Jesus Christ, had died for their sins (Eph. 2:8–10). Nevertheless, the Jewish Christian disciples continued to worship at the Temple, keep the law, and even offer up sacrifices (Acts 21). The parenthetical age of the dispensation of God's sovereign grace, the Church age, is set forth in Acts 15:14–18:

> Simeon hath declared how God at the first did visit the Gentiles, to take out of them a people for his name. And to this agree the words of the prophets; as it is written, After this I will return, and will build again the tabernacle of David, which is fallen down; and I will build again the ruins thereof, and I will set it up: That the residue of men might seek after the Lord, and all the Gentiles, upon whom my name is called, saith the Lord, who doeth all these things. Known unto God are all his works from the beginning of the world.

The phrase, "after this I will return," means that when the tabernacle of David is destroyed (meaning the nation of Israel and Jewish worship including the Temple) and God has completed the calling out of the world a people for His name (the Church, the body of all Christians), Jesus Christ will return and magnify the Jewish nation and rebuild the Temple. According to the very words of James, this will happen only after the Church age has ended and the taking out of the world "a people for his name" has been completed.

Throughout the ministry of Jesus, which lasted for three to three and one-half years, He was asked continually, even by His chosen twelve, ". . . Lord, wilt thou at this time restore again the kingdom to Israel?" (Acts 1:6). The answer to this question was given by Jesus, without any qualification, in Matthew 23:37-39:

O Jerusalem, Jerusalem, thou that killest the prophets, and stonest them which are sent unto thee, how often would I have gathered thy children together, even as a hen gathereth her chickens under her wings, and ye would not! Behold, your house is left unto you desolate. For I say unto you, **Ye shall not see me henceforth, till ye shall say, Blessed is he that cometh in the name of the Lord.**

The conversion of Israel to a belief in Jesus Christ as the Messiah was an important part of the mission of the early Christian disciples between A.D. 30 and 70. Peter and John preached daily at Solomon's Porch on the east side of the Temple to the Jews:

The God of Abraham, and of Isaac, and of Jacob, the God of our fathers, hath glorified his Son Jesus; whom ye delivered up, and denied him in the presence of Pilate, when he was determined to let him go. But ye denied the Holy One and the Just, and desired a murderer to be granted unto you; And killed the Prince of life, whom God hath raised from the dead; whereof we are witnesses.

—Acts 3:13-15

Peter continued to present the answer to Israel's situation:

But those things, which God before had shewed by the mouth of all his prophets, that Christ should suffer, he hath so fulfilled. **Repent ye therefore, and be con-**

verted, that your sins may be blotted out, when the times of refreshing shall come from the presence of the Lord; And he shall send Jesus Christ, which before was preached unto you.

—Acts 3:18–20

Had Israel as a nation been converted by the preaching of Peter and John, and as a people been ready to cry, "Blessed is He that cometh in the Name of the Lord," God would have sent His Son, Jesus Christ, back to reign on David's throne and bring in the Millennium as promised in Revelation 20.

Christians living between A.D. 30 and 70 had every right to expect Jesus to come back in their lifetime. The Epistle of James (A.D. 45) was the first book of the New Testament to be written:

Be patient therefore, brethren, unto the coming of the Lord. Behold, the husbandman waiteth for the precious fruit of the earth, and hath long patience for it, until he receive the early and latter rain. Be ye also patient; stablish your hearts: for the coming of the Lord draweth nigh.

—James 5:7–8

The second and third books of the New Testament to be written were 1 and 2 Thessalonians. Each chapter in 1 Thessalonians has its setting in the return of Jesus Christ:

. . . wait for his Son from heaven, whom he raised from the dead, even Jesus, which delivered us from the wrath to come.

—1 Thessalonians 1:10

For what is our hope, or joy, or crown of rejoicing? Are not even ye in the presence of our Lord Jesus Christ at his coming?

—1 Thessalonians 2:19

... stablish your hearts unblameable in holiness before God, even our Father, at the coming of our Lord Jesus Christ with all his saints.

—1 Thessalonians 3:13

For the Lord himself shall descend from heaven with a shout, with the voice of the archangel, and with the trump of God: and the dead in Christ shall rise first: Then we which are alive and remain shall be caught up together with them in the clouds, to meet the Lord in the air: and so shall we ever be with the Lord.

—1 Thessalonians 4:16–17

For yourselves know perfectly that the day of the Lord so cometh as a thief in the night. For when they shall say, Peace and safety; then sudden destruction cometh upon them, as travail upon a woman with child; and they shall not escape. But ye, brethren, are not in darkness, that that day should overtake you as a thief.

—1 Thessalonians 5:2–4

Second Thessalonians concerns an event, the Abomination of Desolation, that will be committed by a false world messiah, commonly referred to as the Antichrist: "Who opposeth and exalteth himself above all that is called God, or that is worshipped; so that he as God sitteth in the temple of God, shewing himself that he is God" (2 Thess. 2:4).

Some have interpreted the Abomination of Desolation to have occurred when Antiochus Epiphanes of Syria offered a sow on the Temple altar in about 175 B.C., but Jesus still referred to this abomination as being future in A.D. 30 (Matt. 24:15).

Jesus foretold the destruction of the Temple and Jerusalem within the life of the generation of His day (Matt. 24:2,34). Some have suggested that when the Romans destroyed the Temple in A.D. 70, this was the prophesied Abomination of Desolation. However, a careful reading of all the prophecies relating to the Abomination of Desolation show it will occur three and one-half years before the literal return of Jesus Christ to this earth.

The importance of what we have presented so far in this chapter is that just before the return of Jesus Christ when the "man of sin" commits the Abomination of Desolation, what Jesus warned the Jews about will happen.

Then let them which be in Judaea flee into the mountains: Let him which is on the housetop not come down to take any thing out of his house: Neither let him which is in the field return back to take his clothes. And woe unto them that are with child, and to them that give suck in those days! But pray ye that your flight be not in the winter, neither on the sabbath day: For then shall be great tribulation, such as was not since the beginning of the world to this time, no, nor ever shall be.

—Matthew 24:16–21

When the Abomination of Desolation is committed, then only those Jews who immediately flee for their lives will escape. As was the case in the Yom Kippur War of 1973, this ultimate abomination will probably be on a Sabbath. Increasingly, Israel today is restoring observance of Mosaic laws, including strict adherence to Sabbath laws; therefore, some Jews may not be ready to flee, or reticent to flee and break the Sabbath.

The place to which the Jews are directed in Matthew 24 is "the mountains." Other scriptures refer to their hiding place as a place of chambers or the wilderness. Either place could refer to Petra, as this ancient metropolis would fit all descriptions. It is a wilderness; it is a place of chambers; and it is on top of the highest mountain, either in Israel or immediately adjacent to Israel.

As previously noted in this chapter, the earliest Christians did expect Jesus to come back in their lifetime. However, after the destruction of the Temple, the church fathers adjusted their understanding of eschatology. There are a number of extra-biblical dissertations credited to Barnabas, Eusebius, and others expressing a consensus that inasmuch as God created the world and all things therein in six days, the present age would last for six thousand years, and then the Lord would return to bring in the glorious seventh millennium represented by the Sabbath, a day of rest for all mankind (Heb. 4:9).

We are not taking the space to publish these writing credits to the early church fathers, and we are not contending that they were actually written by Barnabas, Eusebius, and the other authors named. Nevertheless, it is apparent from the age of these writings that an evidently large number of believers in the early church, after A.D. 70, thought that Jesus Christ would return soon after A.D. 2000. Edward Gibbons made a study of the doctrines and beliefs of the early church; he concluded in his monumental work, *The Rise and Fall of the Roman Empire,* that the "reigning sentiment" in the early church was that because one day was as a thousand years with God, that Jesus Christ would return with His triumphant saints in two thousand years. Those interested enough may want to research Gibbons' conclusions at the local library. In light of other prophetic fulfillments of our day, we find them extremely interesting.

In the prayer of Moses recorded in Psalm 90, we read that a thousand years with God is as yesterday. Most ministers consider this psalm as referring to the lifespan of man, but a closer reading reveals that it also covers the scope of the lifespan of all mankind. It actually looks forward to the end of man's day and the beginning of the Lord's Day: "Return, O LORD, how long? and let it repent thee concerning thy servants [Israel]" (Ps. 90:13).

Another reference to "one day as a thousand years with God" is in 2 Peter 3:8, but here too it refers to the end of man's day and the beginning of the Lord's Day: "But the day of the Lord will come as a thief in the night ..." (2 Pet. 3:10).

The prophet Hosea may have had the one-day-to-a-thousand-year ratio in mind when he prophesied concerning the return of Israel to the land in the last days. The prophet first looks upon the estate of Israel during a great dispersion:

> For the children of Israel shall abide many days without a king, and without a prince, and without a sacrifice, and without an image, and without an ephod, and without teraphim: Afterward shall the children of Israel return, and seek the LORD their God, and David their king; and shall fear the LORD and his goodness in the latter days.
>
> —Hosea 3:4–5

When Pilate asked the multitude who would accept responsibility for the death of Jesus, a just and innocent man, "Then answered all the people, and said, His blood be on us, and on our children" (Matt. 27:25).

From the genealogy of Jesus in Matthew and Luke, it appears that only Jesus Christ was the sole heir to David's throne. After the death of Jesus, no pretender to the throne of David has arisen. Israel has indeed been many days without a prince, without a Temple, and until recently, without a country.

The prophet Zechariah prophesied about the return of Israel in the last days:

> In that day will I make the governors of Judah like an hearth of fire among the wood, and like a torch of fire in a sheaf; and they shall devour all the people round about, on the right hand and on the left: and Jerusalem shall be inhabited again in her own place, even in Jerusalem.
>
> —Zechariah 12:6

The setting of this prophecy could not be in the Tribulation. It is clearly just before the Tribulation, and we read within the context about the "governors" of Israel, not a prince or a king. In the 1967 war between Israel, Egypt, Jordan, and Syria, the old Jerusalem, the Jerusalem recognized by God, was indeed inhabited again in its own place.

Next let us consider when Hosea predicted the return of Israel:

> Come, and let us return unto the LORD: for he hath torn, and he will heal us; he hath smitten, and he will bind us up. After two days will he revive us: in the third day he will raise us up, and we shall live in his sight.
>
> —Hosea 6:1-2

Applying again the one-day-to-a-thousand-years ratio, the Jews were torn and scattered for almost two thousand years. A growing remnant is returning to the land, waiting for the Lord to completely revive the nations as foretold in Ezekiel 37:1–6:

> The hand of the LORD was upon me, and carried me out in the spirit of the LORD, and set me down in the midst of the valley which was full of bones, And caused me to pass by them round about: and, behold, there were very many in the open valley; and, lo, they were very dry. And he said unto me, Son of man, can these bones live? And I answered, O Lord GOD, thou knowest. Again he said unto me, Prophesy upon these bones, and say unto them, O ye dry bones, hear the word of the LORD. Thus saith the Lord GOD unto these bones; Behold, I will cause breath to enter into you, and ye shall live: And I will lay sinews upon you, and will bring up flesh upon you, and cover you with skin, and put breath in you, and ye shall live; and ye shall know that I am the LORD.

In review, Petra will become of prophetic importance in the day when:

» Israel will become a nation again and win miraculous victories against overwhelming odds. This has occurred.

» A great nation to the north of Israel called Gog in Ezekiel 38–39 will move with a great army over the mountains of Israel to take a "great spoil." Most Bible scholars interpret this nation to be Russia. Even with the breakup of Russia as an empire and its seeming rebirth as a commonwealth, the nation still has many weapons of mass destruction and an increasing danger of mass starvation.

» Israel's flight to Petra will come three and one-half years after the signing of a Middle East comprehensive peace treaty (Dan. 9:27). At the writing of this book, efforts to negotiate this treaty are underway.

» Petra will again loom into prominence when knowledge has increased, along with accelerated communications and travel (Dan. 12). It is claimed by educators that man's knowledge is doubling every two and one-half years; 90 percent of all scientists who ever lived are alive today; man's speed of travel remained constant at thirty miles an hour for fifty-nine hundred years, but in the last ninety years has increased threefold on the ground, twentyfold in the air, and six hundredfold in outer space; in the last ninety years, radio, television, laser, and satellite communications have been developed; in the past fifty years nuclear weapons capable of destroying the world many times over have been made and stockpiled.

» Petra would be readied for its role in the last days when the Roman Empire would be revived and a world government leader would demand that everyone on earth worship him as a god (Rev. 13). On November 11, 1991, Jeane Kirkpatrick, former U.S. ambassador to the United Nations, wrote: "If the Bush Administration has a vision of a New World Order, it is time to share it with Europeans and Americans, because a New World Order is precisely what is emerging on the continent of Europe today. And with minimal American participation." A united Europe, the Revived Roman Empire, will become a world government according to Jeane Kirkpatrick, and this is as the Bible prophecies. A *National Geographic* Internet item dated September 10, 2003, stated in part: "Efforts to protect Petra and its artifacts continue even as tourism grows."

» The Abomination of Desolation that will be the signal for Israel to flee to Petra will come in a time when all the world is working, buying, and selling using code marks and numbers (Rev. 13). The world has just about arrived at this economic stage.

» The January 6, 2009, edition of *WorldNetDaily* reported Henry Kissinger's response to a question about Mr. Obama being the head of an imminent New World Order: "There is a need for a New World Order," Kissinger told PBS interviewer Charlie Rose. "I think at the end of this administration, with all its turmoil, and at the beginning of the next [Obama administration], we might actually witness the creation of a New World Order." In the same interview Mr. Kissinger suggested that Mr. Obama would be the right leader for a New World Order.

At the entrance to Petra is a sign, "A United Nations Heritage Site." In 2007 Petra was designated as ONE OF THE SEVEN WONDERS OF THE WORLD. When I first went to Petra there was one hotel. Today, there are seventy-three hotels, and in November 2008 my tour group could hardly get into Petra because there were wall-to-wall tourists from all over the world.

The preceding and many other prophetic signs in evidence today serve as signals for the ancient city of Esau to prepare for an influx of visitors, the children of Jacob.

ABOMINATION OF DESOLATION

And this gospel of the kingdom shall be preached in all the world for a witness unto all nations; and then shall the end come. When ye therefore shall see the abomination of desolation, spoken of by Daniel the prophet, stand in the holy place, (whoso readeth, let him understand:) Then let them which be in Judaea flee into the mountains: . . . For then shall be great tribulation, such as was not since the beginning of the world to this time, no, nor ever shall be.

—Matthew 24:14–16,21

M any of the Old Testament prophets foretold the sequence of events related to the end of the age, but Jesus chose to quote the prophet Daniel. Daniel was perhaps the best-known of all prophets in the non-Jewish world. He had been a trusted advisor in Nebuchadnezzar's court; he was one of the presidents of Persia, and the Persians built him a mansion and honored him as a great prophet and statesman. The books of Daniel were widely read throughout the known world at that time. Josephus records that Alexander the Great read the prophecies of Daniel. It is probable that the wise men who came from the east to Bethlehem were the Magi, or star prophets, from the cabinet of the king of Persia, or the seven princes of Persia who served in the royal palace (see Est. 1:10,14). By studying the ninth chapter of Daniel, any of the Magi, or any of the princes, would have known the date the Messiah was to be born. And this is possibly why Jesus references Daniel, as he was the most widely read and respected of all the Hebrew prophets.

The Abomination of Desolation is mentioned specifically three times by Daniel:

» "And he shall confirm the covenant with many for one week: and in the midst of the week he shall cause the sacrifice and the oblation to cease, and for the overspreading of abominations he shall make it desolate, even until the consummation, and that determined shall be poured upon the desolate" (Dan. 9:27).

The person mentioned by Daniel who will confirm the covenant with many for one week is generally interpreted to be the prince, or king, of the Revived Roman Empire. He will make a treaty with Israel for one week, evidently honoring the covenant that God made with Abraham which involves the right of his seed to the land God gave Israel. The week for the term of the treaty is not seven days, but seven years, or the seventieth week of Daniel's seventy weeks of years. Jacob worked for Leah a week (seven years) and then had to work for Rachel another week. After three and one-half years, this international political and/or religious figure will stop sacrificial worship, presumably on the Temple Mount in Jerusalem. Today, many of the orthodox and observing Jews are preparing to resume traditional Jewish worship just as soon as possible. The reason given by Daniel for the termination of Jewish worship is for the overspreading of abominations. This person, also called the Antichrist, will demand that everyone in the world worship him as God, and he will sit, or stand, in the Holy Place claiming to be God. To claim to be the Messiah, the Christ of God, is the ultimate abomination. But it is for the overspreading, or for the purpose of demanding everyone in the world worship him as God, that the abomination occurs. Many Jews will not worship this man as God, so evidently his first act is to desolate the Temple Mount and the Holy Place, and then move to kill all the Jews.

» "And arms shall stand on his part, and they shall pollute the sanctuary of strength, and shall take away the daily sacrifice, and they shall place the abomination that maketh desolate" (Dan. 11:31).

The extent of the power and brutality of this man, also called the Beast, is further amplified in Revelation: "And he opened his mouth in blasphemy against God, to blaspheme his name, and his tabernacle, and them that dwell in heaven. And it was given unto him to make war with the saints, and to overcome them: and power was given him over all kindreds, and tongues, and nations. And all that dwell upon the earth shall worship him, whose names are not written in the book of life of the Lamb slain from the foundation of the world. . . . And he doeth great wonders, so that he maketh fire come down from heaven on the earth in the sight of men, And deceiveth them that dwell on the earth by the means of those miracles which he had power to do in the sight of the beast; saying to them that dwell on the earth, that they should make an image to the beast, which had the wound by a sword, and did live. And he had power to give life unto the image of the beast, that the image of the beast should both speak, and cause that as many as would not worship the image of the beast should be killed" (Rev. 13:6–8,13–15).

Although we may not know exactly what the image of the Beast will be, it will doubtless entail a world communication center, else his image could not speak to all the people of the earth demanding that they worship the Beast as God.

The apostle Paul described the Abomination of Desolation thusly: "Let no man deceive you by any means: for that day shall not come, except there come a falling away first, and that man of sin be revealed, the son of perdition; Who opposeth and exalteth himself above all that is called God, or that is worshipped; so that he as God sitteth in the temple of God, shewing himself that he is God" (2 Thess. 2:3–4).

The description of the Abomination of Desolation by Paul corresponds with those of Daniel and Jesus, with the exception that the apostle Paul calls the Antichrist the "man of sin" or "the son of perdition." Instead of this abomination occurring in the Holy Place of the sanctuary, Paul indicates it will occur in the Temple. But the Greek word for temple used by Paul could also be interpreted "holy place."

» "And at that time shall Michael stand up, the great prince which standeth for the children of thy people: and there shall be a time of trouble, such as never was since there was a nation even to that same time: and at that time thy people shall be delivered, every one that shall be found written in the book. And many of them that sleep in the dust of the earth shall awake, some to everlasting life, and some to shame and everlasting contempt. . . . And I heard the man clothed in linen, which was upon the waters of the river, when he held up his right hand and his left hand unto heaven, and sware by him that liveth for ever that it shall be for a time, times, and an half; and when he shall have accomplished to scatter the power of the holy people, all these things shall be finished. ... And from the time that the daily sacrifice shall be taken away, and the abomination that maketh desolate set up, there shall be a thousand two hundred and ninety days. Blessed is he that waiteth, and cometh to the thousand three hundred and five and thirty days" (Dan. 12:1-2,7,11-12).

According to Daniel, the Abomination of Desolation will be near the time when the saved of Israel will be resurrected. It is our understanding of the order of resurrection that the Church, meaning all Christians, will be changed and translated as the seven-year period of Tribulation begins (1 Thess. 4:13-18). The Old Testament believers who died in the faith will be resurrected at the end of the Tribulation when Jesus Christ returns. The unsaved will be raised and judged at the end of the Millennium (Rev. 20:11-15). However, just prior to the resurrection of Israel, the Jews will be scattered, after the Abomination of Desolation, for a time, times, and one-half time. A time, according to the Hebrew calendar, was one year, from one Passover to the next. Again we see that the Jews will be out of the land in hiding for three and one-half years. This time corresponds with the time for the last half of the Tribulation given in Revelation. We will attempt to reconcile the difference between the exact days given by Daniel from the number in Revelation in the next chapter.

Daniel and Jesus both agree that following the ultimate act of abomination, there will be a time of trouble such as the world has never witnessed before. Let us now consider some pertinent information about the Abomination of Desolation.

Who will commit it? It will be an act committed by a world political figure called in the Bible the man of sin, the son of perdition, the prince of the people who shall come, the Beast, and the Antichrist. This man will be aided and abetted by a world religious leader called the False Prophet.

Where will it be committed? It will be committed at the site of the Holy Place, the Temple Mount, Mount Moriah, in Jerusalem. It may or may not be committed inside a new tabernacle or a rebuilt Temple. At the writing of this book, Jordanian (Muslim) guards still have control over the Temple Mount.

When will it be committed? It will be committed in the middle of Daniel's seventieth week, three and one-half years after a comprehensive peace treaty has been signed with Israel by the person who will become the Antichrist.

What will it be? From the scriptures, we can determine the act itself will entail

» The stopping of Jewish sacrificial worship at the Temple site,
» The Antichrist proclaiming at the Holy Place on Mount Moriah, or in the Temple, that he himself is God, the Christ, or Messiah, and
» The Beast will then establish an image on the Temple site that will command everyone in the world to worship it under penalty of death. But . . .

What Is the Desolation?

In Daniel 9:26, the prophet wrote: ". . . unto the end of the war desolations are determined." The last half of the Tribulation will be a time of war and desolation. The following prophecies magnify the extent and scope of these coming judgments:

... I will make the land of Egypt utterly waste and desolate, from the tower of Syene even unto the border of Ethiopia. No foot of man shall pass through it, nor foot of beast shall pass through it, neither shall it be inhabited forty years. And I will make the land of Egypt desolate in the midst of the countries that are desolate, and her cities among the cities that are laid waste. ...

—Ezekiel 29:10–12

O thou daughter dwelling in Egypt, furnish thyself to go into captivity: for Noph [Cairo] shall be waste and desolate without an inhabitant.

—Jeremiah 46:19

The burden of Damascus [oldest city in the world]. Behold, Damascus is taken away from being a city, and it shall be a ruinous heap.

—Isaiah 17:1

And Babylon [modern Iraq], the glory of kingdoms, the beauty of the Chaldees' excellency, shall be as when God overthrew Sodom and Gomorrah.

—Isaiah 13:19

For it is the day of the LORD's vengeance, and the year of recompences for the controversy of Zion. And the streams thereof shall be turned into pitch, and the dust thereof into brimstone, and the land thereof shall become burning pitch.

—Isaiah 34:8–9

... and the mountains shall be thrown down, and the steep places shall fall, and every wall shall fall to the ground.

—Ezekiel 38:20

... hail and fire mingled with blood, and they were cast
upon the earth: and the third part of trees was burnt
up, and all green grass was burnt up.

—Revelation 8:7

... Lebanon is ashamed and hewn down ... And the
people shall be as the burnings of lime: as thorns cut
up shall they be burned in the fire.

—Isaiah 33:9,12

The preceding verses of Scripture are probably not even
one percent of those describing the terrible desolation that will occur in the nations of the world after the
Abomination of Desolation occurs on the Temple Mount.

An interesting comment that seemingly refers to the
Antichrist is found in Daniel 11:44–45:

... tidings out of the east and out of the north shall
trouble him: therefore he shall go forth with great fury
to destroy, and utterly to make away many. And he
shall plant the tabernacles of his palace between the
seas in the glorious holy mountain; yet he shall come
to his end, and none shall help him.

Why, in considering the many great cities of the world,
would the emperor of Planet Earth choose Jerusalem as
his headquarters?

God established Jerusalem to be the capital city of
all the world. It is from Jerusalem that the King of Kings,
Jesus Christ, will rule all nations with a rod of iron. In
Zechariah 14:16 we are informed that during the Kingdom age the leaders of all nations will go to Jerusalem to
honor the King, the Lord of hosts. Therefore, all would-be
world conquerors have desired the city of Jerusalem.

Sennacherib, the great monarch of the Assyrian Empire, tried to conquer Jerusalem, but he failed. Nebuchadnezzar attempted to control Jerusalem while building his own counterfeit Jerusalem—Babylon. Nebuchadnezzar failed, so he destroyed Jerusalem.

Alexander the Great set out to conquer the world. He first marched along the Mediterranean coast to destroy the bases of the Persian navy, and he defeated the vastly superior army of Persia at Issus in Turkey. Then he continued and utterly annihilated Tyre, but when he had intentions to destroy Jerusalem, God spoke to him in a dream and Jerusalem was spared (Josephus).

The Caesars of Rome, a world empire, conquered and held Jerusalem for five hundred years. Muhammed sent his top general, Omar, to take Jerusalem and cleanse the Temple Mount from Roman desecration. The Crusaders were commissioned by the pope to take Jerusalem from the heathens, and these knights from Europe held the city for 150 years. Next, Suleiman the Magnificent from Turkey held Jerusalem in the fourteenth century and rebuilt the wall.

Napoleon of France had designs to be a world ruler. He first landed in Egypt, where he won a great victory over the Marmalukes. Next, he sailed to Israel and disembarked his troops at Acre. The Crusaders had built a castle at Acre that was supported by a double moat system. Napoleon, expecting another easy victory, ordered his troops over the moats. The bodies of fallen French soldiers filled the first moat before the general ran out of men. He loaded the remnant of his army back on his ships and sailed back to France by way of Egypt. Napoleon never set foot in Jerusalem.

In World War II, Hitler had intentions of conquering the world. He first attempted to kill all the Jews in the world, and almost succeeded. He sent his top general, Rommel, racing across North Africa toward Jerusalem; and at the same time, sent his Panzer divisions down through the Balkans toward the Middle East in a pincer attack. But Rommel was defeated and the unexpected protracted war with Russia stopped the German divisions from advancing past Greece.

The past several popes of the Roman Catholic church have had designs on Jerusalem. The Catholic church has never recognized Israel as a nation, and rumors persist that the Vatican would prefer moving to Jerusalem. The United Nations, including the United States, will not recognize Jerusalem as the capital of Israel.

The time is coming when a world ruler, the president of Planet Earth, will make an attempt to make Jerusalem the capital city of all nations. This is one reason why he is called the Antichrist, because only the Lord Jesus Christ will indeed fulfill God's plan and purpose for Jerusalem: "And it shall come to pass, that every one that is left of all the nations which came against Jerusalem shall even go up from year to year to worship the King, the LORD of hosts, and to keep the feast of tabernacles" (Zech. 14:16).

However, when the Antichrist establishes his own tabernacle (headquarters) in Jerusalem and commits the Abomination of Desolation, the Jews are to immediately flee to their designated hiding place, which we believe to be Petra. Then for three and one-half years, terror and desolation will reign upon the earth. "And the nations were angry, and thy wrath is come . . . and shouldest destroy them which destroy the earth" (Rev. 11:18).

The prophet wrote in Zechariah 12:3, "And in that day will I make Jerusalem a burdensome stone for all people. . . ." The reference "*at* that day" means just before the Great Tribulation. "*In* that day" means in or after the

Great Tribulation. Jerusalem is the only national capital that no other nation will recognize. In 2007 the last two nations that still maintained an embassy in Jerusalem moved to Tel Aviv. When U.S. diplomats meet with Israeli diplomats, they have to meet outside Jerusalem in Tel Aviv lest the Muslim nations think the 138United States is recognizing Jerusalem as the capital.

When Jesus Christ returns, every nation will have to acknowledge Jerusalem as not only the capital of Israel, but the capital city of all nations, and every leader of every nation will have to go to Jerusalem to acknowledge Jesus Christ as King of Kings (Zech. 14:17).

THE TIME OF JACOB'S TROUBLE

Important truths of God are often presented in symbolic or allegorical form. Had all the Bible been written in literal language, then it should be obvious that it would have been destroyed centuries ago as the words of madmen.

One such biblical illustration is the flight of the remnant of the Jews from Judea, the area surrounding Jerusalem, to a place of safety especially prepared by God. The flight itself, and the reason for it, are described in symbolic terminology in Revelation. God's messenger told Daniel that his prophecy would be sealed until the time of the end, and the same can be said of many other prophecies. Only in these latter days are we beginning to compare representative prophetic truths with contemporary events. Such is the case with the twelfth chapter of Revelation:

> And there appeared a great wonder in heaven; a woman clothed with the sun, and the moon under her feet, and upon her head a crown of twelve stars: And she being with child cried, travailing in birth, and pained to be delivered. And there appeared another wonder in heaven; and behold a great red dragon, having seven heads and ten horns, and seven crowns upon his

heads. And his tail drew the third part of the stars of heaven, and did cast them to the earth: and the dragon stood before the woman which was ready to be delivered, for to devour her child as soon as it was born. And she brought forth a man child, who was to rule all nations with a rod of iron: and her child was caught up unto God, and to his throne.

—Revelation 12:1-5

Much of what John saw and recorded in the Apocalypse was in the form of visions (Rev. 9:17). We can imagine the apostle watching the unfolding of the story of Revelation 12 in much the same way we would watch a Walt Disney presentation.

The first thing that John saw appear was a great wonder in Heaven. The Greek word for "wonder" is *teras,* but the word used for "wonder" here was *semeion,* which means sign or prophecy. The wonder that John saw was a pregnant woman clothed with the sun, the moon under her feet, wearing a crown of twelve stars. Some interpret the woman to be Mary, the mother of Jesus; others believe she is the Church; but most prophetic scholars agree that the woman is Israel. In Genesis 37, Joseph saw his father Jacob as the sun, his mother Rachel as the moon, and the twelve brothers as stars. This was the entire host of Israel with which God made everlasting covenants, including the bringing forth of the Messiah. Also, in the Old Testament Israel is frequently described as the wife of God, even though at times unfaithful. The man-child is, of course, Jesus Christ who was caught up to Heaven after His resurrection, and He is the only one in the Bible who is destined to rule over all nations with a rod of iron (Rev. 19:5).

Israel to this date has never recognized Jesus as the only begotten Son of God. Israel as a nation is not yet even aware that they have given birth to the Messiah; therefore, no birth pangs have been felt. However, during the Tribulation when Israel will be crying out for the Messiah, the nation will then suffer the pains of birth. In reference to Israel in the last days, we read in Isaiah 66:7–8: "Before she travailed, she brought forth; before her pain came, she was delivered of a man child. Who hath heard such a thing? who hath seen such things?..."

This is the picture that John sees of Israel during the Tribulation, feeling birth pangs after her child has been delivered. Jeremiah explained the first five verses of Revelation 12 as follows:

> For, lo, the days come, saith the LORD, that I will bring again the captivity of my people Israel and Judah, saith the LORD: and I will cause them to return to the land that I gave to their fathers, and they shall possess it. And these are the words that the LORD spake concerning Israel and concerning Judah. For thus saith the LORD; We have heard a voice of trembling, of fear, and not of peace. Ask ye now, and see whether a man doth travail with child? wherefore do I see every man with his hands on his loins, as a woman in travail, and all faces are turned into paleness? Alas! for that day is great, so that none is like it: it is even the time of Jacob's trouble; but he shall be saved out of it.... But they shall serve the LORD their God, and David their king, whom I will raise up unto them.
>
> —Jeremiah 30:3–7,9

The time of Jacob's trouble will be the last half of the Tribulation when the Israelites flee from the land. Jesus said there would be woe to those with child, possibly a symbolic reference to Israel's birth pangs for the Messiah. Jeremiah even saw the men bent over with pain seemingly trying to give birth, a most graphic explanation of Israel's plight as described in Revelation 12. Satan is seen as the red dragon in the form of the Beast empire, ready to do battle with the Lord Jesus Christ when He returns with the armies of Heaven. Not only did Satan attempt to kill Jesus Christ at His birth, but when he sees Israel in pains of birth in expectation of the Messiah, the devil must know that the return of Jesus Christ is near (v. 12).

"And the woman fled into the wilderness, where she hath a place prepared of God, that they should feed her there a thousand two hundred and threescore days" (Rev. 12:6). John at this point in the vision sees a woman (Israel) running into the wilderness, or the mountains, as Jesus instructed. The escape route will not simply lead into a general wilderness, but rather to a particular place, a place prepared by God.

As to the number of Jews who will escape, it would seem this question is partially answered in Zechariah 13:8–9:

And it shall come to pass, that in all the land, saith the LORD, two parts therein shall be cut off and die; but the third shall be left therein. And I will bring the third part through the fire, and will refine them as silver is refined, and will try them as gold is tried: they shall call on my name, and I will hear them: I will say, It is my people: and they shall say, The LORD is my God.

If the number of Jews in Israel at the writing of this book is three million, as commonly reported, then one million will escape. Two million will die in the aftermath of the attempt by the "man of sin" to kill all the Jews. These estimates are, of course, based upon the present number of Jews in the land.

The accounting of time for the duration of Jacob's troubles is as follows:

» "In the midst of the week" (Dan. 9:27).
» "A thousand two hundred and ninety days" (Dan. 12:11).
» "The thousand three hundred and five and thirty days" (Dan. 12:120.
» "A time, times, and an half" (Dan. 12:7).
» A thousand two hundred and threescore days" (Rev. 12:6).
» "A time, and times, and half a time" (Rev. 12:14).
» "Forty and two months" (Rev. 11:2).
» "Forty and two months" (Rev. 13:5).

During this period of three and one-half years, great desolations over the earth will occur and destroy cities, vegetation, birds, cattle, and millions of people around the world. Even the oceans will be polluted and marine life will die. A world dictator will proclaim himself to be God, and he will have control over the nations for forty-two months. The Jews in Israel who escape will be hidden in a place of safety, prepared by God.

As we consider the possibility of Petra being the place where Israel would wait for the coming of Messiah, there would be sufficient water for a million people. Not only does Ain Musa provide a good water source, but there are dozens of other springs and wells in the area. Food could be a problem, but if God could take care of three million Hebrews wandering in the desert for forty years, He can certainly take care of a million Jews waiting in a relatively safe place. Also, even though the soil is rocky in Petra, it is very rich. On one visit it had just rained a couple of days previously, and almost overnight the entire ground was covered with gorgeous desert tulips.

In reconciling the time factor for the "time of Jacob's trouble," forty-two months would be approximately 1,260 days, or 1,277 days by our present calendar. A time, times, and a half time would be approximately forty-two months, or 1,260 days. But like Easter, the Jewish holy days, including Passover, could fall two or three weeks earlier or later than the previous year. This could be the reason the time is extended in Daniel 12:11 by thirty days. However, this would not explain the extension of seventy-five days, or two and one-half months. The shorter time of 1,260 may somehow be related to the observation by Jesus, "And except those days should be shortened, there should no flesh be saved . . ." (Matt. 24:22). The extra thirty days could be time taken in bringing the Jews from Petra and regathering the rest scattered through the nations. Then, the extra forty-five days could be needed for the setting up of the Lord's kingdom as indicated in Revelation 20:4. But these are only speculations on our part and may not be applicable at all. Nevertheless, we can be sure that there is a reason for the time differential of seventy-five days.

And there was war in heaven: Michael and his angels fought against the dragon; and the dragon fought and his angels, And prevailed not; neither was their place found any more in heaven. And the great dragon was cast out, that old serpent, called the Devil, and Satan, which deceiveth the whole world: he was cast out into the earth, and his angels were cast out with him. And I heard a loud voice saying in heaven, Now is come salvation, and strength, and the kingdom of our God, and the power of his Christ: for the accuser of our brethren is cast down, which accused them before our God day and night. And they overcame him by the blood of the Lamb, and by the word of their testimony; and they loved not their lives unto the death. Therefore rejoice, ye heavens, and ye that dwell in them. Woe to the inhabiters of the earth and of the sea! for the devil is come down unto you, having great wrath, because he knoweth that he hath but a short time.

—Revelation 12:7–12

It is generally concluded by the majority of Bible scholars that Satan was an exalted angelic being in God's Kingdom who was named Lucifer, meaning "the bright and shining one." God must have made Lucifer, because God made all things. It is possible that all angels of God have names, but only three are named in the Bible: Gabriel, Michael, and Lucifer. Sin is rebellion against God, and Satan became the original sinner when he decided to raise his own throne (kingdom) above the stars of God (Isa. 14). Angels are often referred to as stars in the Bible. In Scripture we read of the angels who kept not their first estate and of the angels of Satan. Where did Satan's angels come from? The only reasonable answer to this question is that Lucifer drew one-third of the angels of Heaven over to him in rebellion against God (Rev. 12:4). We are informed in Ephesians that Christians have inherited heavenly places in Jesus Christ, and it has been suggested that when the members of the Church reach the number equal to the number of the angels that fell, to replace the fallen angels in Heaven, the Church will be translated, or raptured.

Since Lucifer fell from his exalted position in the Kingdom of God because of pride and ambition, there has been war in the heavens. How else can we explain the novas, supernovas, black holes, and chaos even in our own solar system as reported by our space probes. The war in the heavens will end in victory for God when Michael leads his angels against Satan and his angels. They will be cast out of the heavens down to earth, and as John saw in the vision, this will be a terrible time for all people on earth living at that time.

And when the dragon saw that he was cast unto the earth, he persecuted the woman which brought forth the man child. And to the woman were given two wings of a great eagle, that she might fly into the wilderness, into her place, where she is nourished for a time, and times, and half a time, from the face of the serpent.

—Revelation 12:13–14

These two verses again describe the flight of Israel to a place of safety as the Abomination of Desolation takes place. Yet, the woman with child still pains to be delivered. The scene is also described by Isaiah:

Like as a woman with child, that draweth near the time of her delivery, is in pain, and crieth out in her pangs; so have we been in thy sight, O LORD. We have been with child, we have been in pain, we have as it were brought forth wind; we have not wrought any deliverance in the earth; neither have the inhabitants of the world fallen. . . . Come, my people, enter thou into thy chambers, and shut thy doors about thee: hide thyself as it were for a little moment, until the indignation be overpast. For, behold, the LORD cometh out of his place to punish the inhabitants of the earth for their iniquity: the earth also shall disclose her blood, and shall no more cover her slain.

—Isaiah 26:17–18,20–21

During the last half of the Tribulation, the time of Jacob's trouble, a remnant of Israel will hide for forty-two months until the Lord comes to bring peace out of war, order out of chaos:

And the serpent cast out of his mouth water as a flood after the woman, that he might cause her to be carried away of the flood. And the earth helped the woman, and the earth opened her mouth, and swallowed up the flood which the dragon cast out of his mouth. And the dragon was wroth with the woman, and went to make war with the remnant of her seed, which keep the commandments of God, and have the testimony of Jesus Christ.

—Revelation 12:15–17

It seems apparent that John here was attempting to give us a clue that the hiding place of Israel would be Petra. As we have previously noted from several sources, the floods of Petra are legendary. As far as the "wings of a great eagle" are concerned, this was the terminology used by the black Jews from Ethiopia when they were flown by huge passenger jets from Ethiopia to Jerusalem in the summer of 1991. It is quite possible that many of the Jews will be flown from Jerusalem to Petra by helicopters and airplanes. When I was in Petra last, we were told that the government of Jordan planned to build a large airport adjacent to the city.

After one-third of the Jews escape, it is apparent the Antichrist moves to kill all the Jews left he can find, including the 144,000 Jewish evangelists mentioned in Revelation 7. However, from Revelation 14:1–5, it would seem that they will be translated to Heaven.

For the remaining months of the time of Jacob's trouble, the remnant of Israel waits in hiding for the coming of Messiah. To these people Jesus gave the following instructions:

> Wherefore if they shall say unto you, Behold, he is in the desert; go not forth: behold, he is in the secret chambers; believe it not. For as the lightning cometh out of the east, and shineth even unto the west; so shall also the coming of the Son of man be.
>
> —Matthew 24:26–27

THE HIDING PLACE

After World War II, the book entitled The Hiding Place related how many Jews were hidden in a special place in Amsterdam so they would not be arrested and executed by the German Gestapo. All down through the centuries of the Diaspora, the Jews scattered through the nations have needed hiding places. They have been driven from city to city, nation to nation, hated and persecuted, just as the prophets foretold.

After World War II, most nations (with the exception of the Arab bloc) sympathized with Israel in establishing a homeland for the Jews. But while the United Nations has come to the aid of nations like South Korea that have become victims of aggressive intents, the U.N. has not come to Israel's aid when attacked in three wars by overwhelming aggressive forces.

Increasingly, world opinion has changed from a sympathetic position in favor of Israel to a neutral, or even a critical, position. The United States has been the only consistent and helpful friend of Israel in time of need; yet, even Americans are beginning to question the reason for that nation's continued financial aid. The United States now would prefer to see some kind of peaceful solution to the Arab-Israeli controversy. Thus, the pressure behind a comprehensive conference to bring an end to U.S. commitments. The biggest bone in the throat of the

Arab world is Jerusalem and the Temple site. Muhammed is said to have ascended to heaven from the rock over which the Dome of the Rock stands, and Abraham is believed by the Muslims to have also sacrificed Ishmael on that rock. According to an AP news release dated October 25, 1991, Israel will never permit Jerusalem to be a bargaining chip at any future peace conference. This point of contention is mentioned with an end-time setting in Zechariah 12:3: "And in that day will I make Jerusalem a burdensome stone for all people...."

Although great efforts are being made to effect a peaceful settlement of the 4,000-year-old Arab-Israeli controversy, Jeremiah said such efforts will fail: "And these are the words that the LORD spake concerning Israel and concerning Judah. For thus saith the LORD; We have heard a voice of trembling, of fear, and not of peace ... it is even the time of Jacob's trouble..." (Jer. 30:4–5,7).

Looking behind the peace efforts and the peace treaty of Daniel 9:27, Zechariah wrote: "Behold, the day of the LORD cometh, and thy spoil shall be divided in the midst of thee. For I will gather all nations against Jerusalem to battle..." (Zech. 14:1–2).

Behind all the peace efforts in the Middle East, the children of Ishmael and the children of Esau remain determined to eliminate Israel and drive the Jews into the sea. A news report, dateline Nicosia, Cyprus, dated October 12, 1991, describes the centuries-old hatred that simmers beneath the surface:

The commander of Iran's Islamic Revolutionary Corps said Sunday that Muslim states should form an Islamic army to liberate Jerusalem, the official Islamic Republic News Agency reported. Rezale's remarks came on the second day of a conference in the Iranian capital that brought together Palestinian and other groups from the Arab and Muslim worlds.

For the aforementioned reasons, if the nation of Israel is to be saved until the end of the Tribulation, a hiding place will be required for the remnant. The Bible declares it; political developments shaping up in the Middle East project it. But it will not be as it was in A.D. 70, in the Spanish Inquisition, or even during World War II. The Jewish persecution during the coming Tribulation will be the result of worldwide action. A world dictator will be in power. There will be no place of escape for the Jews except in that hiding place mentioned in Isaiah 26:20–21: "Come, my people, enter thou into thy chambers, and shut thy doors about thee: hide thyself as it were for a little moment, until the indignation be overpast. For, behold, the LORD cometh out of his place to punish the inhabitants of the earth for their iniquity. . . ."

Let us consider the clues given in the Bible as to where the Jews will be hiding for three and one-half years.

Clue No. 1—Accessibility: According to the prophecy of Jesus in the Olivet Discourse, the Jews will not have time to pack their suitcases or even a picnic lunch. Therefore, the place where God will hide them will of necessity be near Israel. Jesus also said in Matthew 24:19–21: "And woe unto them that are with child, and to them that give suck in those days! But pray ye that your flight be not in the winter, neither on the sabbath day: For then shall be great tribulation, such as was not since the beginning of the world to this time, no, nor ever shall be." Petra is 120 miles southeast of Jerusalem, and while this would be an extremely difficult journey for the Jews, it would not be impossible. While it may be possible that some of the Jews may be transported in an airlift operation, the warnings about the sufferings and dangers of the journey by Jesus indicates land movement. Jesus also mentioned the hardships that would be involved in a winter flight. Winters in Israel are not usually very severe, temperatures normally in the forty-five to sixty degree range. Only about once in every ten years does it get cold enough to snow in Jerusalem. Petra is an entirely different climate, extremely hot in summer and very cold in winter, often with heavy snow. This factor is another indication that Petra will be Israel's place of refuge.

Clue No. 2—Geography: The Scriptures are very plain in that the Jews hiding place will be in the mountains. The warning is, ". . . flee to the mountains. . . ." The highest point in Israel is 3,963 feet in elevation, and the mountains in Israel are generally high, rolling hills that would provide little protection. The highest mountains in Jordan are in the Petra area. Certainly, Petra would qualify, as it is in a rugged, mountainous area.

Clue No. 3—Political: The hiding place of the Jews needs to be a place that would be difficult for the forces of Antichrist to reach. The Antichrist will know everything about everyone, and no man or woman will be able to buy or sell without his mark or number. We read in Revelation 13:7, ". . . and power was given him over all kindreds, and tongues, and nations." However, there will be one nation that will be released from Antichrist's control, and strangely enough, this will be a country next door to Israel—Jordan. We read in Daniel 11:41, ". . . but these shall escape out of his hand, even Edom, and Moab, and the chief of the children of Ammon."

The identity of this nation and ruler is not difficult to determine. The boundaries of Edom, Moab, and Ammon form exactly the boundaries of modern Jordan, and the chief, or ruler of Jordan, lives in the capital, Amman, just like Daniel prophesied. When Winston Churchill in 1921 drew a line that separated Jordan from Israel, and made the statement that Israel would have no authority over the land east of the Jordan and Dead Sea, little did he realize that he was fulfilling prophecy.

As to why Jordan will escape out of the hands of Antichrist is not entirely clear from this point in time. Jordan claims ownership of the West Bank, including Jerusalem. Perhaps the autonomy of Jordan will be one of the considerations in the treaty that the Antichrist will negotiate, and he will honor his commitments to Jordan, but not to Israel. Herod was an Edomite who became a Roman citizen in order to be the king of Judea, a Roman province. Perhaps the Antichrist may have a similar racial identity, and this is why Jordan will not be under Antichrist's control during the last half of the Tribulation. We also should remember that the vast armies of Antichrist will not be gathered in Israel until the very last of the Tribulation, so his overall military power in that area until that time may be limited. In any event, Jordan will be the one nation in the world that will be released from the Antichrist kingdom, and in the last half of the Tribulation, Israel will flee through the old territories of Moab and Edom to Petra. God will doubtless have a hand in this matter in order that this will be made possible. We read in Daniel 4:17, ". . . the most High ruleth in the kingdom of men, and giveth it to whomsoever he will, and setteth up over it the basest of men." Even during the reign of Antichrist, God will still be in control. But this prophecy is another reason why Petra will be the place of refuge for Israel during the Tribulation.

Clue No. 4—Availability: Next, let us consider just how big this hiding place will have to be for those Jews to make good their escape. If we can determine the number of Jews that will be housed during the last three and one-half years of the Tribulation, this will help us in our search, because we will then know how big it will have to be. Not all Jews will escape to the place of refuge, because we are informed in many scriptures that only a remnant will be saved out of the "time of Jacob's trouble." The percentage is given in Zechariah 13:8–9: "And it shall come to pass, that in all the land, saith the LORD, two parts therein shall be cut off and die; but the third shall be left therein. And I will bring the third part through the fire, and will refine them as silver is refined, and will try them as gold is tried: they shall call on my name, and I will hear them: I will say, It is my people: and they shall say, The LORD is my God."

There are approximately three million Jews in Israel today, so we must look for a place that will hide at least a million people. As we have already noted, most tourists who go to Petra actually see only about 5 percent of the city. Altogether, it is a vast complex of cave dwellings, covering a twenty-square-mile area. Some of these dwellings will hold up to one thousand people. Therefore, Petra will certainly be big enough. It will not have to be vacated; it is still practically empty, with only a few Bedouins living in a few of the caves near the Ciq. So far, all the clues we have considered point to Petra as the "hiding place" for Israel during the last half of the Tribulation.

Clue No. 5—Geological: From a geological standpoint, we are informed by the prophet Isaiah that the hiding place of Israel at the time the Lord comes to judge the earth and bring in His Kingdom on earth will be a place of chambers, or we could say caverns or caves. We read in Isaiah 26:20–21: "Come, my people, enter thou into thy chambers, and shut thy doors about thee: hide thyself as it were for a little moment, until the indignation be overpast. For, behold, the LORD cometh out of his place to punish the inhabitants of the earth for their iniquity: the earth also shall disclose her blood, and shall no more cover her slain."

The "indignation" referred to by Isaiah is doubtless the Abomination of Desolation. So, as it were for a little moment, Israel will be hidden in chambers until the Lord comes to destroy the armies of Antichrist at the battle of Armageddon. In addition to the thousands of caves in Petra, the entire area abounds in natural caverns. We quote from *The Sarcophagus of an Ancient Civilization:* "The etymology of the name 'Horites' throws light upon their social and national character. If, as many suppose, the name 'Horite' is derived from the Hebrew word *hor,* meaning 'hole' or 'cave,' then the gentilic derivative *Hori,* and its plural *Horim,* would signify Troglodytes, or cave dwellers. This derivation seems highly probable in view of the numerous caves and caverns with which Edom abounds. Burckhardt reports having seen in his travels . . . 'many natural caverns.' . . . Doughty tells of exploring 'limestone caverns' not far north of Petra near a place called Khidal. . . . While Palmer considers the caves and artificial caverns which he saw at al-Barid, a suburb to the north of Petra, as the dwelling of an ancient people."

Petra more than qualifies as a place of chambers for Israel's hiding place when the Lord comes. Israel's hiding place is also described as being in the wilderness. In the Bible, "wilderness" refers to an uninhabited region, or a desert, a place that is inaccessible except to certain types of animals. *Cruden's Concordance* says: "The wilderness of Paran was in Arabia Petrea." The "wilderness" of Paran in which the children of Israel wandered is referred to in Genesis 21:21; Numbers 10:12; 13:3,26; 1 Samuel 25:1. We read in Numbers 10:12: "And the children of Israel took their journeys out of the wilderness of Sinai; and the cloud rested in the wilderness of Paran [or Petra]." There are many areas of wilderness referred to in the Bible, and while the references to Petra as a wilderness do not prove that it will be the hiding place, in conjunction with it being a place of caverns is a very important clue.

Clue No. 6—Zoological: Zoo means a collection of animals, birds included. In references given previously in this study, the names of the birds and animals that would inhabit Petra during the period of its desolation are given. Petra, being a place of high cliffs and caves, is a natural home for owls and eagles. From Scripture, we know that there were eagles that made their homes in the cliffs. We read in Obadiah 1,3–4: " . . . Thus saith the Lord GOD concerning Edom; . . . The pride of thine heart hath deceived thee, thou that dwellest in the clefts of the rock, whose habitation is high; that saith in his heart, Who shall bring me down to the ground? Though thou exalt thyself as the eagle, and though thou set thy nest among the stars, thence will I bring thee down, saith the LORD."

Opposite the Ciq upon entering Petra is one of the more beautiful buildings, the Treasury Building. Toward the top of the facade and in the center is an eagle carved in stone. At another location is an eagle monument. We quote from the book *Petra* by Browning: "Carved into the rock on the other side of the water tunnel is a square panel from which a very imperial eagle looks away from you. The Eagle Monument is probably a votive niche."

We read also in Jeremiah 49:16–17: "Thy terribleness hath deceived thee, and the pride of thine heart, O thou that dwellest in the clefts of the rock, that holdest the height of the hill: though thou shouldest make thy nest as high as the eagle, I will bring thee down from thence, saith the LORD. Also Edom shall be a desolation: every one that goeth by it shall be astonished. . . ."

It is significant that we read of Israel's flight in Revelation 12:14: "And to the woman were given two wings of a great eagle, that she might fly into the wilderness, into her place, where she is nourished for a time, and times, and half a time, from the face of the serpent."

Clue No. 7—Logistical: We have already dealt with this matter somewhat, but let us consider the history of the Jews as far as logistics are concerned. Some biblical historians estimate that as high as two and one-half million Jews came out of Egypt. For forty years these Jews wandered in a barren, waterless, fruitless desert that is so desolate it is difficult to understand how even a survival expert could live more than a few weeks. Yet these people survived for forty years and went into the Promised Land.

The Babylonian captivity era of seventy years was a difficult time for the Jews, yet they survived. In A.D. 68 the Romans trapped one million Jews in Jerusalem, closed the gates to the city, and shut off all water and food supply sources, and for two years they survived. Jerusalem finally had to be taken by a massive military assault by the finest troops in the Roman army. And then, what about Masada? For over two years, from A.D. 72 to 73, several hundred Jews defied the Romans at this fortress. They were completely surrounded with no escape route. This flat rock is about one thousand feet high, approximately one-half mile long, and one-quarter mile wide. There is no water supply, no grass—it is totally barren. Beyond human comprehension, they not only survived, but fought the Romans for two years, and finally the survivors committed suicide rather than surrender.

During the last nineteen hundred years, the Jews have been scattered into all nations and endured persecution, torture, and death in almost every country they have lived. In World War II, Hitler killed from four and one-half to six million Jews, depending upon the source. Yet, the Jews have survived and are still fighting enemies that are forty times their own number. Therefore, we do not have to worry about logistics while the Jews are in Petra. After all they have been through, Petra will be a piece of cake. And in any event, God will look after them as He has always done in the past.

Clue No. 8—Military: According to Isaiah, the city of Bozrah (now Buseirah—*Baker's Bible Atlas,* p. 70), north of Petra on the King's Highway, will figure prominently in the battle of Armageddon and the Lord's return to present Himself to Israel as their Messiah. Bozrah was an important city in the Edomite kingdom, second only to Petra. It is located twenty-five miles south of the southern end of the Dead Sea, about halfway to Petra. That Bozrah will be the southern anchor point at the battle of Armageddon is foretold in Isaiah 34:5–6,8: "For my sword shall be bathed in heaven: behold, it shall come down upon Idumea, and upon the people of my curse, to judgment. The sword of the LORD is filled with blood, it is made fat with fatness, and with the blood of lambs and goats, . . . for the LORD hath a sacrifice in Bozrah, and a great slaughter in the land of Idumea. For it is the day of the LORD's vengeance, and the year of recompences for the controversy of Zion." This is the Bozrah in Edom, not the ones in Syria or Iraq.

Isaiah continues to prophesy that after the "day of the Lord's vengeance," Israel will possess all of Edom forever. Isaiah 63:1–4 describes the appearance of Jesus Christ at Bozrah at the victorious termination of Armageddon to be a Savior to His people, Israel: "Who is this that cometh from Edom, with dyed garments from Bozrah? this that is glorious in his apparel, travelling in the greatness of his strength? I that speak in righteousness, mighty to save. Wherefore art thou red in thine apparel, and thy garments like him that treadeth in the winefat? I have trodden the winepress alone; and of the people there was none with me: for I will tread them in mine anger, and trample them in my fury; and their blood shall be sprinkled upon my garments, and I will stain all my raiment. For the day of vengeance is in mine heart, and the year of my redeemed is come."

We read in Revelation 19:13 that at Armageddon the vesture of Jesus Christ will be dipped in blood, and in verse fifteen John saw Him at Armageddon as one treading the winepress. According to Revelation 14:20, the battle of Armageddon will stretch along a front 1,600 furlongs, or 176 miles. It is 176 miles from Megiddo to Bozrah. The forces of Antichrist will be stopped at Bozrah and not be able to reach the Jews' hiding place in Petra.

Bozrah, being in a less defensive position than Petra, has been overrun and destroyed many times. In the 1920s the natives of Bozrah were almost decimated by cholera. It is also interesting that Ezion-geber has become Aqaba, Philadelphia has become Amman, but Bozrah has kept its biblical name.

I have in the past, in traveling southward along the King's Highway, passed through Bozrah. Recently, guides are reticent to go through the city because of extremely rough and perilous roads. However, Bozrah still remains today a city of several thousand people, ready to fulfill its greatest role, the meeting place of Jesus Christ and the refugees from Israel who have been waiting in Petra for the Messiah. This in itself is a miracle, proving again the infallibility of God's written Word and the certainty of the more sure Word of prophecy.

Clue No. 9—Scriptural: The plain message of Scripture is that Petra will be Israel's hiding place for the last half of the Tribulation. Psalm 60:1,9–12 states plainly that after God has regathered Israel, they will have a time of great trouble, but the Lord will preserve them in the strong city of Edom, which can be no place but Petra: "O God, thou hast cast us off, thou hast scattered us, thou hast been displeased; O turn thyself to us again. . . . Who will bring me into the strong city? who will lead me into Edom? Wilt not thou, O God, which hadst cast us off? and thou, O God, which didst not go out with our armies? Give us help from trouble: for vain is the help of man. Through God we shall do valiantly: for he it is that shall tread down our enemies."

God even gave a heathen prophet, Balaam, a prophecy concerning the possession of Petra by Israel when the Lord God reigns on David's throne: "He hath said, which heard the words of God, and knew the knowledge of the most High, which saw the vision of the Almighty, falling into a trance, but having his eyes open: I shall see him, but not now: I shall behold him, but not nigh: there shall come a Star out of Jacob, and a Sceptre shall rise out of Israel, and shall smite the corners of Moab, and destroy all the children of Sheth. And Edom shall be a possession, Seir also shall be a possession for his enemies; and Israel shall do valiantly. Out of Jacob shall come he that shall have dominion, and shall destroy him that remaineth of the city" (Num. 24:16–19).

We read also in Isaiah 16:1: "Send ye the lamb to the ruler of the land from Sela to the wilderness, unto the mount of the daughter of Zion." The remainder of the chapter concerns Israel's hiding from the Antichrist in Moab and Edom, and in verse fourteen a specific period of "three years" is foretold: "But now the LORD hath spoken, saying, Within three years, as the years of an hireling, and the glory of Moab shall be contemned, with all that great multitude; and the remnant shall be very small and feeble."

WHO ARE
THE PALESTINIANS?

Since Israel became a nation again in 1948, there have been more than fifty treaties agreed to by various countries involved, including the Palestinians, to try to bring peace between the various factions fighting for that tiny piece of land. So far at the writing of this update, not a single treaty has held. Those attempting to negotiate a peace settlement between the Jews and the Palestinians have ignored the biblical reasons for this continuing conflict.

When Esau met Jacob on his way to the Promised Land, it would have appeared that their controversy was resolved and all was forgiven. Subsequently, the descendants of Jacob were in Egypt for four hundred years. After Moses led the Israelites out of Egypt, having multiplied to a couple of million or more, the first enemy that was encountered was Amalek, the king of the Amalekites. Amalek was Esau's grandson (Gen. 36:12). Amalek led an army against Moses and the children of Israel in an attempt to keep the Israelites from claiming the land that God has given to them in his covenant with Abraham (Exod. 17:8–13). As we learn from the ancestral records of the present-day Palestinians, they appear to be descendants of both the Edomites and Amalekites, both races descendants of Esau. We read in Exodus 17:15–16: "And Moses built an altar, and called the name of it Jehovah-nissi: For he said, Because the LORD hath sworn that the LORD will have war with Amalek from generation to generation."

The next controversy that Moses and the children of Israel had with the descendants of Esau was when they attempted to pass by Petra and go through Edom on the way to the Promised Land. Again, the descendants of Esau attempted to keep Israel from claiming their birthright, which Jacob had taken from his brother.

The long-standing wars during the time of the judges, and later the kings of Israel and Judah, have already been referred to in previous chapters.

About 600 B.C., the Babylonian Empire expanded east and west. Judah was threatened, and in desperation made a mutual assistance treaty with their hated enemies, the Edomites. Instead of coming to Judah's assistance, the Edomites joined the Babylonians and helped to destroy Jerusalem and the Temple. This act again demonstrated the deceitful and treacherous nature of the Edomites.

By the rivers of Babylon, there we sat down, yea, we wept, when we remembered Zion. We hanged our harps upon the willows in the midst thereof. For there they that carried us away captive required of us a song; and they that wasted us required of us mirth, saying, Sing us one of the songs of Zion. How shall we sing the LORD's song in a strange land? If I forget thee, O Jerusalem, let my right hand forget her cunning. If I do not remember thee, let my tongue cleave to the roof of my mouth; if I prefer not Jerusalem above my chief joy. **Remember, O LORD, the**

children of Edom in the day of Jerusalem; who said, Rase it, rase it, even to the foundation thereof.

—Psalm 137:1–7

It was common practice in those days to racially mix a conquered nation to destroy identity and the will to resist occupation. The well-educated Jews and their best physical specimens were taken to Babylon in captivity. Then the Edomites were moved out of Petra into Judah. The Nabateans, descendants of Ishmael's grandson Naboth, moved up from the south in Arabia and took over Edom. This was prophesied in Obadiah 19: "And they of the south shall possess the mount of Esau; and they of the plain the Philistines: and they shall possess the fields of Ephraim...."

The Philistines possessed the land of Ephraim in the Assyrian captivity, and the Nabateans from Arabia during the Babylonian captivity possessed Edom, including Petra. The Edomites lived in Judah. After seventy years of Babylonian captivity, a remnant of the Jews were allowed to return to rebuild Jerusalem and the Temple. The Jewish builders had to work with their armaments by their side to fight the Edomites who were trying to prevent the rebuilding.

The return of the Jews from Babylonian captivity to rebuild Israel was a long and difficult process. National revival was also complicated by the continual march of armies through the land from Egypt and Syria. Although under the Macabees, Israel regained some of its former glory, the Romans came into the Middle East and the nation was again under the authority of a foreign government. Josephus recorded the activities of the Edomites (called Idumeans by the Romans) during this period. The Romans could not place Jews in governmental positions, so they appointed Edomite stooges to supervise needed police and civil functions. The Herods were Edomites. When the Romans destroyed Jerusalem and the Temple in A.D. 70, the majority of the Jews were either killed, sold into slavery, or fled to other countries. The Edomites, having nothing to fear from the Romans, stayed in the land and became the ancestors of present-day Palestinians.

Josephus recorded in many places in both of his books the evil deeds of the Edomites in Israel. In *Wars of the Jews,* book 4, chapter 5, is just one incident of Edomite madness and cruelty:

> ... nor did the Idumeans spare anybody; for as they are naturally a most barbarous and bloody nation ... and acted in the same manner as to those that supplicated for their lives as those that fought them, insomuch that they ran through those with their swords who desired them to remember the relation there was between them, and begged of them to have regard to their common temple ... the outer temple was overflowed with blood; and that day, as it came on, saw eight thousand five hundred dead bodies there. But the rage of Idumeans was not satisfied by these slaughters; but they now betook themselves to the city [Jerusalem], and plundered every house, and slew everyone they met.

Josephus said that the Edomites were an exceedingly mad and cruel people with an intense hatred for the Jews. The historian concluded that this hatred, when unleashed, knew no reason or bounds.

Philo of Alexandria wrote of the Edomites:

> ... this earthly Edom, being excessively indignant, will

threaten us with irreconcilable wars . . . the earthly
Edom thinks it right to blockade the heavenly and royal road of virtue, and the divine reason blockades his
road, and that of all who follow his opinions. . . . For the
diseases of the soul are truly not only difficult of cure,
but even utterly incurable.

— *The Works of Philo,* pp. 172–173

It may seem incomparable to the civilized mind that the
Edomite king, Herod, would order all Jewish babies under two years old in Bethlehem and the surrounding area
to be killed (Matt. 2:16). But going back in the history of
the PLO (Jewish confrontations since 1920), we find case
after case and incident after incident where Palestinian
terrorists have killed Jewish school children purposely.
In Israel today, when you see a group of school children,
you will see an armed guard watching over them. PLO
suicide bombers seek out gatherings of teens to kill, or
mothers with babies and young children. The targeting
of children by suicide bombers has been noted more and
more by the news media. The tactics of the PLO and its
related terrorist organizations seem to correspond in every detail with those of the Edomites. This is probably no
coincidence as the intense hatred of Esau and his descendants, the Edomites, are ingrained within the character
of Palestinians.

In recent years, terrorists have hijacked our planes,
murdered our pilots and passengers, hanged our U.N.
representatives, killed over two hundred of our Marines
in Lebanon, bombed our embassies in Africa, bombed
with casualties the *U.S.S. Cole* in Yemen, and murdered
over three thousand innocent civilians in the September 11, 2001, tragedy. In addition to the billions of dollars in damage and the millions of Americans thrown out

of work due to the destruction of the Twin World Trade Towers, now taxpayers are having to pay another $21 billion for damages to New York City.

Certainly, not all of the terrorists who committed these deeds were Palestinians. Yet, the Palestinians have provided the initiative, the cause, the fervor, and the lies that have attracted their religion and blood brothers to join the carnage. The United States is deeply mired in this incredible war that began four thousands years ago when Jacob stole Esau's blessing and birthright. This murderous feud will in due course bring the armies of all nations against Jerusalem (Zech. 14:2). Where will the armies of the United States be when this happens?

CONCLUSION

The preponderance of biblical, historical, and prophetic evidence portends that in Petra the birth pangs of Israel will finally cease when the Jews realize that the man-child for whom they have yearned for so long was born in Bethlehem of Israel in the days of King Herod the Edomite:

> And it shall come to pass in that day, that I will seek to destroy all the nations that come against Jerusalem. And I will pour upon the house of David, and upon the inhabitants of Jerusalem, the spirit of grace and of supplications: and they shall look upon me whom they have pierced, and they shall mourn for him, as one mourneth for his only son, and shall be in bitterness for him, as one that is in bitterness for his firstborn.
>
> —Zechariah 12:9–10

So that we Christians would not be ignorant of that day, the apostle Paul wrote to us as stated in Romans 11:25–27:

> For I would not, brethren, that ye should be ignorant of this mystery, lest ye should be wise in your own conceits; that blindness in part is happened to Israel, until the fulness of the Gentiles be come in. And so all Israel

shall be saved: as it is written, There shall come out of Sion the Deliverer, and shall turn away ungodliness from Jacob: For this is my covenant unto them, when I shall take away their sins.

And so all Israel who escapes from the time of Jacob's trouble will see Jesus Christ, the One who was crucified in Israel, raised again from the grave, appearing before them in all His majesty and glory. This will be the Revelation witnessed by the apostle John: "Behold, he cometh with clouds; and every eye shall see him, and they also which pierced him: and all kindreds of the earth shall wail because of him. Even so, Amen" (Rev. 1:7).

We read of that glorious day when Jesus Christ returns and ascends the throne of His father David in Jerusalem to rule all nations with a rod of iron:

> The stone which the builders refused is become the head stone of the corner. This is the LORD's doing; it is marvellous in our eyes. **This is the day which the LORD hath made; we will rejoice and be glad in it. . . . Blessed be he that cometh in the name of the LORD: we have blessed you out of the house of the LORD.**
> —Psalm 118:22–24,26

In that day, all Israel, every Jew, will be saved; not because of the law, the covenants, or their racial ancestry. They will be saved only because they will believe on the Son of God who died for their sins. This is the only way the sinfulness, the ungodliness of Jacob can be taken away. It will be then that every man, woman, and child of the house of Israel and the house of Judah will shout:

Blessed Is He That Cometh in the Name of the Lord!!

But what about the Palestinians and other Arabic racial entities that survive the Tribulation and continue to live in the land which God gave Israel? Will there be a Palestinian state then? NO! From the Euphrates to the Nile there will be only the Greater Israel, but the Lord Jesus Christ will reign in Jerusalem and other racial entities living on the land will enjoy the blessings of the Messiah through Israel. Then finally the descendants of Esau and the descendants of Jacob will live together in peace and prosperity.

> So shall ye divide this land unto you according to the tribes of Israel. And it shall come to pass, that ye shall divide it by lot for an inheritance unto you, and to the strangers that sojourn among you, which shall beget children among you: and they shall be unto you as born in the country among the children of Israel; they shall have inheritance with you among the tribes of Israel. And it shall come to pass, that in what tribe the stranger sojourneth, there shall ye give him his inheritance, saith the Lord GOD.
> —Ezekiel 47:21–23

When Israel was to become a nation again, God said He would give the world a sign: three world leaders were to die within one month (Zech. 11:8). On April 12, 1945, President Roosevelt, who was against Israel becoming a nation, died suddenly. On April 28, 1945, Benito Mussolini, a co-partner with Hitler in exterminating six million Jews in Europe, was killed by his own countrymen. On the last day of April 1945, Adolph Hitler committed suicide.

Since May 14, 1948, when Israel became a nation, it has fought three major wars against odds of sixty–to–one or more. In addition, the nation has survived against internal terrorism—Palestinian suicide extremists who have killed Israelis in their synagogues, businesses, and buses. Israel has maintained a standing army where every boy and girl has had to serve in the military and financially maintain those forces larger than nations with forty times greater populations. Israel has also had to fight Palestinian armies to the north in Lebanon and in areas like the Gaza Strip that have been armed by other Muslim nations. Yet, Israel has survived as promised in Zechariah 12:6.

On the ninth day of the Jewish month of Av, the nation of Israel remembers the past. The following events all occurred on that day:

» Israel forbidden to enter the Promised Land
» First temple destroyed
» Second temple destroyed
» Decree to expel Jews from England
» Decree of Spanish Inquisition
» World War I began
» Hitler ordered Jewish extermination
» Jewish settlers expelled from Gaza

More than fifty peace treaties have been signed between Israel and its neighbors, yet there is no peace. The efforts of the past seven presidents of the United States and the two hundred–nation membership of the United Nations have not been successful in bringing peace between Israel and its Islamic neighbors. The reason is that God said there would be continual war between the descendants of Jacob and the descendants of Esau until the Messiah ruled as King of Kings over all nations.

Israel has yet to face the invasion of Gog prophesied

in Ezekiel 38 and 39; the abomination of desolation that Jesus Christ foretold, with the massacre of two-thirds of the population; and the period of three and one-half years spent in Petra, explained in detail in this book.

But as the Apostle Paul explained in Romans 11, God has not cast away His people, and the day is coming when Christ returns and their eyes will be opened, their ears will hear the gospel, and their stony hearts will be replaced with one of love for their Saviour Jesus Christ. Then the prophecy in Amos 9:11–15 will become their eternal history:

> In that day will I raise up the tabernacle of David that is fallen, and close up the breaches thereof; and I will raise up his ruins, and I will build it as in the days of old: That they may possess the remnant of Edom, and of all the heathen, which are called by my name, saith the LORD that doeth this. Behold, the days come, saith the LORD, that the plowman shall overtake the reaper, and the treader of grapes him that soweth seed; and the mountains shall drop sweet wine, and all the hills shall melt. And I will bring again the captivity of my people of Israel, and they shall build the waste cities, and inhabit them; and they shall plant vineyards, and drink the wine thereof; they shall also make gardens, and eat the fruit of them. And I will plant them upon their land, and they shall no more be pulled up out of their land which I have given them, saith the LORD thy God.

For the Jewish remnant
who will be waiting for Messiah in Petra

A MESSAGE OF HOPE
TO EVERY JEW IN THE
TIME OF JACOB'S TROUBLE

(Written by a Jew who found the Messiah)

My name is Earl Werner. I was born of Orthodox Jewish parents, an heir of the covenants that God made with Abraham, Isaac, and Jacob. I am writing to you, my Jewish brethren by race, to share with you a message of hope as you await deliverance from your hiding place, which appears from the words of the prophets of Israel to be Petra, also called "the rock," "Mount Seir," and "Sela" (Isa. 16:1).

My Jewish friend, I know that you and many more of our countrymen, possibly numbering in the millions, have been betrayed and suffered much in physical hardships and the loss of loved ones. Our leaders were deceived, or pressured, into accepting a man who claimed

[170]

to be our long-awaited Messiah. This traitor negotiated a covenant, or peace treaty, with Israel in which certain promises were made guaranteeing the religious freedom of the Jews and the security of our land from foreign aggressors. This treaty was to last for seven years, but after three and one-half years, this false messiah broke his promise and moved to kill every Jew in Israel. Why? Because he is a tyrant and the devil's servant. If you have already read this book to this point, then you are aware of the details of this act of abomination.

As a young boy, I went to synagogue services regularly. I went to Talmud Torah, but never did I hear about the time of immense tribulation you and others are experiencing. Several of our prophets wrote to warn that this time of great trouble would come upon Israel in the last days. Jeremiah in the thirtieth chapter of his book wrote about it; Daniel wrote about it in the twelfth chapter of his book; other prophets, including Joel and Ezekiel, wrote about it. Now you surely understand just what they were referring to in their prophecies.

When you read this, the writer will have already been called to Heaven to be with the Lord. I will have died a natural death, possibly because of my age, or translated from earth to Heaven in a great catching away at the time the false messiah signed the treaty with Israel. Christians in looking forward to this miraculous event called it "the Rapture." Perhaps three or four years ago you heard reports of the sudden disappearance of millions of people out of all nations. At that time, 144,000 Jews suddenly became believers in "Yeshua" as the true Messiah and Savior and began preaching in His Name and converting thousands and millions in all nations to a like faith. Then this vicious and wicked man, also called the "son of perdition" and the "man of sin" stopped Jewish worship at the Temple Mount and launched an attack on Jerusalem and surrounding cities to kill everyone. It was then that you and others, about one-third of Israel, as prophesied by the prophet Zechariah in chapter thirteen, made your way to Petra. Perhaps some of the 144,000 Jewish believers in Yeshua directed you to the place you are now. Surely by now you have seen all these things happen. I know they will happen because they are foretold by the prophets.

If you go back and read again the scripture verses mentioned in this book, as well as the last several chapters of Zechariah, you will come to an understanding concerning the days and events which still are ahead of you. There will be terrible desolations and tribulations until Yeshua comes. Armies from all nations will be gathered together in Israel for the last great battle, called Armageddon. It will be then that Yeshua will come with the armies of Heaven in much the same manner that Israel expected Him to come almost two thousand years ago before the Temple and Jerusalem were destroyed, then Yeshua, the Lord Himself, will meet you and all the remnant of Israel at Bozrah, just about twenty-five miles to the north, to lead you all back home. The false messiah and this so-called holy man will be cast alive into the "lake of fire" in much the same manner as those who rebelled against God and worshipped the golden calf, when Israel came out of Egypt, were swallowed up by the earth. You can read about this in Isaiah 66, and if you have a Christian New Testament, read Revelation 19. You might be reticent to be instructed by a Gentile or read the Christian New Testament, but it is foretold in Isaiah 28:11, "For with stammering lips and another tongue will he speak to this people."

I refer you again to Daniel 12:11–12: "And from the

time that the daily sacrifice shall be taken away, and the abomination that maketh desolate set up, there shall be a thousand two hundred and ninety days. Blessed is he that waiteth, and cometh to the thousand three hundred and five and thirty days."

You know now how many more days you have to wait for the coming of Messiah. But my dear Jewish brother in the flesh, you do not have to wait for His coming. You can believe on Him and be saved right now. You can read in Psalm 22 and Isaiah 53 that the Messiah had to die first, offer Himself as a sacrifice, for our sins. The greatest decision I ever made in my life was to accept Yeshua Hamasheoch, my Lord Jesus Christ, as my own personal Savior. It is written in the Christian New Testament, Romans 11, that when Yeshua returns, all Israel alive will be saved by believing in Him, not only as Messiah the King, but as Messiah who died for their sins. What a glorious day this will be. Then the promises made to Israel through Abraham, Isaac, Jacob, and David will be fulfilled. Jerusalem has become the capital city of the world. All the leaders of the nations will come to Jerusalem to worship the Lord God of Israel, whom I know as Yeshua, Jesus the Christ. Then there will be peace on earth, no more war, no more crime, no more tribulation for Israel. This is all in the books of the prophets. Read Zechariah 14 again, as well as Isaiah 65–66.

Yeshua said that His coming again with the armies of Heaven would be as lightning. You and your fellow Israelis in Petra will not have to guess as to His identity. There is now no reason to be misled again by a false messiah. Look for the nail prints in His hands, the marks of His crucifixion. Another scripture from the New Testament reads: "Behold, he cometh with clouds; and every eye shall see him, and they also which pierced him: and all kindreds of the earth shall wail because of him. Even so, Amen" (Rev. 1:7).

Spread the good news so that every Jew waiting in Petra for deliverance will be ready for Yeshua's coming!